ENCOUNTERS WITH THE BIBLE

USE AND AUTHORITY IN THE CHURCHES

BY ALLAN GLEASON

WITH A FOREWORD BY WALTER FARQUHARSON

96

Wood Lake Books
Inc

Editing: Jim Taylor and Tim Faller
Page layout: Tim Faller
All illustrations by the author

Canadian Cataloguing in Publication Data

Gleason, Henry Allan, 1917–
    Encounters with the Bible

    ISBN 0–929032–21–7

    1. Bible—Evidences, authority, etc.
2. Bible—Inspiration. 3. Bible—Use I. Title.
BS480.G44 1991   220.1'3   C91–091331–5

Published by
Wood Lake Books Inc.,
Box 700, Winfield, BC,
Canada V0H 2C0

Printed in Canada by
Hignell Printing Ltd.,
Winnipeg, MB, R3G 2B4

CONTENTS

Foreword *by Walter Farquharson* 5

Preface 7

CHAPTER 1
Authority and Use 9

CHAPTER 2
Two Churches 11

CHAPTER 3
Molding Ministers 25

CHAPTER 4
Springfield's Past 43

CHAPTER 5
New Alignments 55

CHAPTER 6
The Evangelical Heritage 67

CHAPTER 7
Modern Evangelicalism 79

CHAPTER 8
Communication Failure 95

CHAPTER 9
The Changing Bible 107

CHAPTER 10
Academia and the Bible 121

CHAPTER 11
The Secular Bible 129

CHAPTER 12
The Bible in Conflict 139

CHAPTER 13
Two Views on Authority 149

FOREWORD

When a family gathers, or when good friends come together to tell stories and hear "the latest" from one another, sometimes there is experienced a special opening up of shared living. This sharing helps make sense of a great variety of experiences and pieces of knowledge. Someone tells a story, and hearers say "Of course, now it comes together. Now it makes sense! Now I know why Jim hasn't been able to see that possibility. Now I know why Rita and Marlene always seem to speak past one another without understanding what each other has been saying. Now I know."

Whether it is a controversy over human sexuality, or some economic issue, or how we read the Bible, or what we see as the place of Jesus Christ, or how we define faithfulness—the problems of communication probably arise out of our history and our histories. We need to know the communities that gave us birth, that nurtured and challenged us, that prepared us, well or poorly, to meet the challenges of our age. Those communities, in preparing us, made it easier or harder for us to speak in such a way that others would recognize our language and understand the meanings we had actually intended in our words.

Within church and society today, ample evidence indicates that there is much miscommunication and misunderstanding. Often our reactions to this reality have been to blame or accuse those whose "blindness," sin or stubbornness prevents them from seeing *our* truth. Unless we develop new tools for understanding we will continue to shout at, over, and past one another. And not God, gospel, nor the art of human communication will have been served.

Allan Gleason has provided a tool to help many begin, or to effectively continue, the uncovering of our story—who we are and how we came to be the way we are. This book, *Encounters with the Bible,* uses a community, a set of personalities, and a variety of reportings that are not so much fictional as they are stereotypic. Gleason also uses generalizations and with broad sweeps of his sociologist/historian/religionist's brushes, he creates an intriguing and significantly enlightening backdrop against which we may view the unfolding struggles in our churches around issues of scriptural authority and interpretation.

This is the work of one who understands and loves the church and its people. Allan has an appreciation of the conservative evangelicals and the mainliners and their subtypes. He celebrates their strengths, names some of their contradictions and peculiarities, and he powerfully shows the divergent paths they have developed out of their common heritage of protestant evangelicalism. His analysis illustrates the nature and role of community and congregational Sunday Schools in creating this common heritage and our secularized Bible.

Protestant evangelicalism, says Gleason, "...fostered a lay distrust of the organized church at the same time it built a society-wide allegiance to the Bible. The fringes of evangelicalism trivialized their Bible and reinforced their distrust."

Protestant evangelicalism created a secularized Bible and the task of Christian education is to desecularize it. "The secularized Bible is fragmented. The surviving fragments are haphazardly selected. Out of context they are prey to twisting and misshaping. To correct this distortion, the Bible must be seen as a whole, as a canon."

This statement, for example, resonates with my own experience: "The Bible is thoroughly secularized by being subordinated to the demands of the culture, and by being forced to support the culture. Our culture has taken possession of the Bible, and will not easily tolerate any challenge to its use."

As Gleason reminds us, "The reformation legacy of the Bible as weapon continues to haunt us today." This author calls us to see the Bible as having a reconciling function and a function of "guiding reconciled Christians as they seek, in fellowship, to be faithful."

Thoughtfully, critically and imaginatively used, Allan Gleason's captivating book will serve effectively the ministries of reconciliation and faithfulness-seeking. It is a valuable contribution to us all at a time when we engage in discussions about the authority and interpretation of Scripture.

WALTER FARQUHARSON
MODERATOR
THE UNITED CHURCH OF CANADA

PREFACE

In my study is a long shelf of books dealing with the nature, authority, and interpretation of scripture. I have read them all, and many others like them. I go back to them frequently; they address issues that I continue to ponder.

There is, not surprisingly, a great deal of reworking of the same ideas, the same arguments, and the same counter-arguments. But I also find that certain matters are largely overlooked or downplayed.

One of those is the many ways the Bible actually figures in the life of a local church, and how this varies from church to church. This cannot be told effectively in the context of theological argumentation, the usual medium in books on the subject. Its natural vehicle is story.

Story has to be specific, and in this case, doubly so. I was fortunate to be able to pick, for the core of my story, a pair of churches and ministers that are so much alike. The two churches are in the same town and serve as nearly the same constituency as such churches ever do. Their pastors, G. Whitefield Finney and Wesley Chalmers, are about the same age and have had about the same amount of experience in the ministry; they come from similar small towns. They are representative of the best in their circles. If you can see behind their religious differences, you will find that they are much alike in personality.

That makes my task of writing easier and the contrast clearer for the reader. Both United churches and Bible churches are changing; if I had picked ministers a generation of two apart there would be additional differences, interesting, perhaps, but not our present concern. I know women in the United Church ministry who would be excellent examples, but again, comparing a woman with a man would introduce an extra factor of a very subtle sort. We do not want to get enmeshed in any sort of *avoidable* difference, anything that would divert from the main focus—their use of the Bible. In a scientific context, it would be called "controlling for other factors."

As much alike as Finney and Chalmers are, there are some inevitable differences. Though from similar towns, the two ministers come from different "sides of the tracks," but that is part of what it means to be United Church and Bible Church in many places. So accounting for some of these entailed differences is part of the task.

Telling a story for a purpose requires that the storyteller be selective.

I have given attention to some details that in another context would seem irrelevant, and I have omitted much. I have emphasized the similarities and differences that underlie different attitudes and beliefs about the Bible, or that arise out of those attitudes and beliefs, and reveal something about them. I have indicated some of the historic roots, since only in our shared traditions can our likenesses and differences be understood.

There has been a temptation, not always successfully resisted, to idealize just a little. I am occasionally mildly critical. In both I have tried to be fair and even-handed.

When I occasionally drop objectivity and make some suggestion or give an interpretation, it is addressed to The United Church of Canada and the United Church of Christ. As a current member of one and a long-time member of the other, I have the right *and* the duty to make such suggestions—but nothing more than suggestions. All I ask is that they be received as such, seriously made by one who has thought for many years about the Bible and its place in the church. I must allow members of other churches to judge for themselves whether my suggestions are worth consideration in their situation.

I think I have something to say to evangelicals also. I do not, of course, presume to make any suggestions to them. At least, they can learn something about one kind of "mainline" thinking, and they can see how their position looks to one outside who has some acquaintance (probably imperfect) with their ways.

I must acknowledge the help, over half a century, of many pastors, lay leaders, "ordinary lay people," and congregations from a hundred or more church fellowships who in some way, large or small, have helped me understand both their faith and mine. For this book, my deepest thanks go to the churches, clergy, and people of Springfield. But that must be shared with many other communities which have helped me in similar ways, and so have aided me in understanding Springfield also. No community can be understood by looking at it alone, however thoroughly it is examined.

Behind all that must be gratitude to our common Lord who has made my experience in the churches one of fellowship. I trust he will accept this as a small effort to extend and deepen community, and to help his people understand their, and their neighbors', encounters with the Bible and with him.

ALLAN GLEASON
PASSION WEEK, 1991

AUTHORITY AND USE

The Bible is central in the life and faith of the Christian community. This is a fact widely recognized across the whole church, but few are satisfied with stating it this way. "Central" seems too weak and a little vague. Most would prefer something more precise.

Among the words used to achieve that precision are "trustworthy," "reliable," "infallible," "inerrant." All are intended to define the Bible's "authority." Unfortunately, no single statement using any of these words is acceptable to every Christian. The result is a great deal of discussion, much of it polemic. From time to time it breaks down into bitter battles, within and between churches.

Most of the debate about "authority" is theological. It tends, therefore, to deal with "authority" in theological contexts. The debate focuses on how the Bible should control our thinking about God and the world, about humanity and its problems, about Jesus Christ and salvation, and about the church and its task. It has to do with convictions and with information, with truth versus falsehood, often with black and white.

The issues are important, and the debate—so long as it remains constructive—is valuable. But it is also limiting.

Look again at my opening statement: "The Bible is central in the life and faith of the Christian community."

While usual statements about the authority of the Bible say a great deal more than this, they also say something less. "Central" speaks of a more general use of the Bible. It not only controls our thinking, it pervades our existence. It is part of our environment. The words of the Psalm can just as well address the Bible as it addresses God:

> Whither shall I go from thy spirit? Or whither shall I flee from thy presence? If I ascend up into heaven, thou art there: if I make my bed in hell, behold, thou art there. (Psalm 139:7–8)

The Bible is read in the churches, and the sermon is normally based on it. But much more than that: the language and at least some of the content of prayer reflect the Bible, as do hymns, anthems, creeds, and everything liturgical. "Do this in remembrance of me" carved on the communion table or a lamb in a stained glass window is an easily recognized bit of Bible. A stylized fish has biblical roots too, but less direct. How many more symbols, not so easily identified, go unrecognized?

So to catch the full significance of the Bible we must look at both use and authority. At both intentional and incidental use. At the Bible as part of our environment.

These things cannot be completely separated. Much discussion of authority attempts to disentangled it from many related matters. But Christian people accept the authority of the Bible, in part, because it is familiar and helpful—even in ways that have nothing to do with "authority." They accept it also because it is inseparable from so much in their environment. In the context of the church, we must look at use and authority *together*.

The ever-presence of the Bible is not restricted to the church. Consider a poster proclaiming some Hollywood figure as "Star of Stars." The poster itself would not appear on a church bulletin board; it panders to a non-biblical notion of success and prestige. Yet that phrase is patterned on "King of Kings," a biblical expression. It has been transferred into an entirely foreign context, and whatever biblical message it might have has been utterly diluted. But it stands as a small reminder of biblical influences far beyond the church.

It also carries a second message: much that is biblical has become so commonplace that we easily overlook its roots. That is true even when it has not been completely secularized, like "Star of Stars." We need to sharpen our eyes and ears to take in the full extent and nature of the use of the Bible, particularly in our own church.

One essential way to understand something familiar is to compare something much less familiar. It will help to look at two different ways the Bible is used within the church. The church is more diverse than most of us realize. At the same time there are some unities that we do not recognize. We need not only to understand a little better our own use of the Bible, but equally to understand that of other Christians around us.

In the local churches, in their worship and other weekly activities, the centrality of the Bible shows most clearly. So that is where we must begin, the place from which we must view wider patterns in the churches.

TWO CHURCHES

M y travels have frequently taken me to the town of Springfield. It has always been my practice to go to my own church every Sunday when I am home, and to whatever church is available when I am away. So my first weekend in Springfield I went to Central United Church, likely the most similar to my home church. I felt right at home there.

On my next trip to Springfield, an old friend of my mother discovered I was in town and invited me to a Sunday meal "right after church." I felt the polite thing would be to go to church with her family, and so was introduced to Lighthouse Bible Church. It was different from my home church, of course. Actually, I found a few things I always wished for in United churches, like the unfeigned cordiality shown to strangers.

Since then, when in Springfield, I have divided my attendance more or less evenly between the two churches. As I have become acquainted with them and with many of the people in each, I have been impressed by the similarities and the differences. They are an ideal pair to exemplify the contrasts that I have seen in so many other places.

C entral United Church is an old and venerable congregation, mostly of people who have been raised in the United Church. It occupies an old and venerable building. Its life centers in its services of worship every

Sunday morning at eleven o'clock. For as long as anyone can remember, the services have been at eleven o'clock, and that seems comfortably right.

The service itself is built about the reading of Scripture and preaching. Most Sundays, three passages are read: one from the Old Testament; one from the Epistles, Acts, or Revelation; and one from the Gospels. All three biblical selections (and the Psalm said together by the congregation) are specified in the lectionary. The lectionary ensures a comprehensive coverage of the Bible over a three-year cycle. It binds the Old Testament to the New, and the Letters to the Gospels. It ties the worship service to the church year, from Advent through Christmas, Easter, Pentecost, and so on. The lectionary is a symbol of shared biblical faith across the wider church. Several other churches in Springfield follow the lectionary also. If United Church members check with their Catholic and Lutheran neighbors, for example, they find that pretty much the same Scripture passages have been read.

In his preaching, the Rev. Wesley Chalmers usually picks up a theme from one of these lectionary readings. Most often he chooses something from the Gospel portion; frequently he brings in something from one of the other passages. Each week he prepares by reading the passages assigned for the Sunday, and then asking himself, "*What is the good news in these passages, for this day, this place, and these people?*" To develop the message, he uses personal experiences, anecdotes, appropriate quotations, and allusions to a wide range of literature. He may even weave in a joke, if it really helps to make a point.

The sermon cannot, of course, cover every aspect of the Christian message every Sunday. But most Sundays it covers some part of it. Chalmers hopes, over the weeks, to give a proclamation as rounded and complete as possible. His aim is not just to proclaim the good news in general, but to tie it to the life and struggles of that people on that day and in that place.

To build that kind of sermon, week after week, is not easy. Chalmers' chief materials are the Bible and his own pastoral experience. Both must be thoughtfully and prayerfully considered, in relation to one another. There is good reason for combining the offices of pastor and preacher.

As a denomination, the United Church has concerns for social justice. When Chalmers can tie one of those to one of the readings for the day, he very likely will. Finding such ties is one part of the question:

"What is the Gospel in these passages, for this day and its struggles, this place and its failings, and this people and their potentials?" Some Sundays, the Gospel—in a narrow, conventional view of the Gospel anyway—seems to be displaced by some social justice concern. But it is only for one Sunday, not over the weeks.

Sometimes, too, place has to be made for some internal program or project of the church. The Sunday which launches the annual financial campaign is the most troublesome. Chalmers finds it difficult to preach the good news as he would like, or even to bring out some justice concerns as compellingly as he would like, when he must sell the budget to the people. But again, this is a single Sunday; with skill and care it can be made to fit into a longer-term plan of proclaiming the Gospel in all its aspects.

L ighthouse Bible Church occupies a more modest building off the main street in Springfield, a block or two from Central. It is a young and vigorous congregation with an aggressive program of reaching out to new people. Most of its members have an intense loyalty, but few have had this  loyalty very long. Its life, too, centers in worship: the Sunday morning service at eleven o'clock—that's when people expect worship to be, and that is when it is easiest to attract new people—*and* the Sunday evening service at seven o'clock, *and* the Wednesday night prayer meeting.

Both Sunday services are built around the reading of Scripture and preaching. Pastor G. Whitefield Finney usually preaches from a single passage, freely chosen for that service. It can be from any part of the Bible. Many in the congregation open their Bibles and follow the reading. They keep them open through the sermon. Finney will, from time to time, call attention to a specific verse or phrase within a verse.

The morning and evening services are different, however.

At the morning service, the preaching is often "expository." That is, it follows through the passage in detail, attempting to make clear the meaning of the text, piece by piece. Some members take notes. Others occasionally underline a phrase in their Bibles or put a brief notation in the margin. Finney cites parallel or related biblical passages, and makes the connection quite explicit. He rarely uses non-biblical allusions; any anecdotes illustrate quite directly the point being made. The preaching at this service seems to be directed primarily to the converted. It often takes the form of argument in support of a point of doctrine—or against some concept considered, in this church, to be incorrect. Very few doctrinal errors are considered minor; if an interpretation is wrong it is decisively wrong. The church assumes that every member should hold to a comprehensive system of sound doctrine. Preaching in the morning service has a central function of building and maintaining that system.

Like Rev. Chalmers, Pastor Finney fits his morning sermons into an on-going program, but his planning takes a different direction. His framework is more like an outline of systematic theology. He tries to cover every aspect of orthodox doctrine, and to tie the individual doctrines together. That seems to be what the people want, and what motivates their note taking or the underlining in their Bibles.

For this same reason Finney frequently links a point in a sermon to a verse he considers pivotal. Among his few dozen constantly quoted favorites—a sort of canon-within-the-canon—are:

...being justified freely by his grace through the redemption that is in Christ Jesus: whom God hath set forth to be a propitiation through faith in his blood. (Romans 3:24–25)

But God commendeth his love toward us, in that, while we were yet sinners, Christ died for us. (Romans 5:8)

Moreover, whom he did predestinate, them he also called: and whom he called, them he also justified: and whom he justified, them he also glorified. (Romans 8:30)

For by grace are ye saved through faith; and that not of yourselves: it is the gift of God. (Ephesians 2:8)

Frequently, a morning sermon at Lighthouse is devoted to eschatology, the doctrine of the end-times. Finney presents an intricate, consistent, and comprehensive scheme built out of verses from Ezekiel, Daniel, and

Revelation. Then he fits into that scheme numerous other verses, from here and there. He gives a detailed chronology. He takes the names appearing in the text as codes, and identifies each one, often with some contemporary person or nation.

Such a sermon is designed to show that things going on around us today were precisely foretold in Scripture as events just before the final drama begins to unfold. These "signs of the times" include wars and rumors of wars, social disintegration, and increasing personal immorality. The vision of things to come—soon—make these catastrophes and warnings of catastrophes, for Finney and his congregation, signs of hope.

E vening services at Lighthouse are less doctrinal. They are announced as being "evangelistic." The preaching is directed to the "non-Christian," that is, to the person who has not made a commitment—or not one of the sort expected at Lighthouse Bible Church. It is designed to encourage such a decision. Indeed, the sermon almost invariably builds up to a direct appeal for decision *tonight.*

The evening preaching is no less biblical than the morning, but is tied to a different set of texts. These are some of Finney's favorites:

> For whosoever shall call upon the name of the Lord shall be saved. (Romans 10:13)
> To him give all the prophets witness, that through his name whosoever believeth in him shall receive remission of sins. (Acts 10:43)
> Behold, I stand at the door and knock: if any man hear my voice, and open the door, I will come in to him, and will sup with him, and he with me. (Revelation 3:20)
> For God so loved the world, that he gave his only begotten Son, that whosoever believeth in him should not perish, but have everlasting life. (John 3:16)

The sermon usually starts from such a text, and returns frequently to it. The text may be repeated a dozen times. But there is much less detailed exposition, and even less bringing in of parallel texts. The intended audience is presumably not yet adept at flipping pages to find Bible passages.

The two churches really have three different kinds of sermons. On any given Sunday, Chalmers' morning sermon at Central United Church will almost always have the strongest pastoral emphasis. The morning sermon at Lighthouse Bible Church will have the strongest instructional emphasis, and the evening message the strongest evangelistic emphasis. But all three qualities are usually present, to some extent, in all three sermons.

Both pastors would agree that all three—nurture of members, teaching of the faith, and proclamation of the good news—*should* be present in every sermon. They interpret these somewhat differently, though, and assign different priorities. Each might be a little dubious about the other touching all three bases adequately.

Interestingly, their styles come together most closely when preaching at funerals. The custom of a full sermon at a funeral has pretty well died out at Central, much to Chalmers' relief. Instead, he usually gives a much briefer meditation. But recently an elderly member requested what she thought of as a traditional funeral. The funeral sermon is disappearing too at Lighthouse, but more slowly. Both pastors realize that this is the occasion when preaching must be overwhelmingly pastoral. Their differences are minimal in their understanding of pastoral ministry.

Each preacher works hard and skillfully at making sermons well organized and properly flowing. But their sermons are crafted on different patterns. The differences are hard to state, but quite evident to any perceptive listener.

In Finney's expository preaching, much of the coherence is provided by the text, as attention shifts from phrase to phrase through it. Chalmers uses a much wider variety of rhetorical devices to ensure the cohesive structure of his sermons.

Perhaps the most striking difference is in predictability. When I first get a worship bulletin, I usually look at the Scripture lessons listed and at the sermon title, and then try to guess what the preacher will do with that material. In United churches I miss more often than I hit. Time after time, the pastor takes a direction that had not crossed my mind.

In churches like Lighthouse, catchy sermon titles are less in vogue, and often there is no title in the church bulletin—if indeed there is a church bulletin. But when the Scripture is announced and read, I make my guess. I usually come pretty close, and sometimes I can fairly well foresee the salient points and how they will be organized. Not always, but often.

Delivery is conspicuously different. At Central, the preacher, in a gown and stole, stands in the pulpit, a box-like structure with an open door to the rear. He reads the sermon, feet firmly in place (or fidgeting unseen!). That it is read is evident—though from long practice, Chalmers is able to maintain intermittent, but effective, eye contact with the congregation.

At Lighthouse, Finney, in a business suit with a handkerchief smartly tucked into his breast pocket, starts behind the pulpit. As he makes a point, he steps to one side or the other. When he really gets worked up, he may be away from the pulpit as much as he is behind it. His gestures are much more dramatic than Chalmers'. He may leave his open Bible on the pulpit, or he may pick it up and carry it with him. He does not read the sermon. He may have an outline tucked inconspicuously into the Bible, but nothing more. Often he does not even have that; the text itself provides the outline. He leafs through the text as he announces a parallel verse, and he repeatedly gestures for attention to the Book in his hand. His preaching gives the impression of being more spontaneous than that at Central.

The two pastors have probably spent about the same amount of time in sermon preparation. But Chalmers prepares one sermon each week; Finney at least two.

Lay members read the Scripture in the morning service at Central. Sometimes they use the Revised Standard Version, sometimes one of the "freer," "modern" translations: the Good News Bible, the New English Bible, or the Jerusalem Bible. They will probably begin reading more and more from the New Revised Standard Version.

At Lighthouse, they are just switching to the New International Version. Until now they have always read from the traditional King James. When Finney quotes from memory, it generally is still the old familiar translation; it will take a while for that shift to be made. That is why the pivotal verses I quoted above were in KJV form.

There may be just a touch of prejudice in these choices of translations. The NIV was at first advertised as a good sound "evangelical" version. That commended it to one church, and did the opposite to the other.

Actually, it is a very good translation, with only an occasional detail that anyone could possibly criticize as doctrinal bias.

On the other hand, the Good News Bible was designed to convey the overall meaning to people who have little background in Bible. It is better for that than for detailed, word-by-word study. The NIV has its priorities the other way; it is good for phrase-by-phrase exegesis, but best for people who know their way around in the Scriptures.

The difference in choice of translation reflects the difference in preaching style and preaching objectives in the two churches, more than it does difference in doctrine. All of these, in turn, reflect the difference in background and education of the two pastors.

The Rev. Wesley Chalmers has a B.A. (*cum laude*) degree from a respected university, majoring in English with a minor in history. This was followed by an M.Div. degree from a prestigious seminary. The study of the Bible was central in the seminary, but always in the context of a much broader education. His church gives him some time for continuing education. He has used that time each year, for the 15 years he has been in the pastorate, to further his skills in counseling, in hospital visitation, and in liturgy.

Pastor G. Whitefield Finney graduated from a four-year Bible School—hardly known outside his church circles—with a Th.B., 15 years ago. He tries to attend a major Bible conference for pastors each year, but it is sometimes difficult to get the time off. Last year he was asked to speak at a conference, and that made it easier.

As in most Bible schools, Finney had a series of intensive courses on each major book or group of books in the Bible. He started his career as a pastor knowing the Bible intimately. Diligent study, mostly on his own, has continually strengthened that command. He can, on demand, sketch the outline of each book in some detail. For each book he can identify and quote the key verses. For almost any matter of faith or practice that comes up, he has a store of crucial texts, and, often, a well-established way of applying each. If none of the standard texts fits the question, he can usually think of one that does. In knowledge of Bible content he is far ahead of Chalmers, who in many cases would have to dig through a concordance to find a needed passage.

Finney's command of the Bible has earned him recognition among similar churches for many miles around. He receives more invitations to lead special Bible studies than he can take on.

By contrast, the theological seminary gave Chalmers a far broader background, much stronger in Church history, liturgics, and history of doctrine. Chalmers can critique Barth, Bultmann, and the liberation theologians at a level Finney can hardly follow. Modern doctrinal movements are Chalmers' special interest. Unfortunately, his congregation understands nothing of this material and cares less, so Chalmers can hardly hint at any of this in his preaching or teaching. It is not all loss, however. Every so often it helps him catch himself before he puts some unsupportable but attractive idea into a sermon.

Moreover, he has been asked to lead a theological reflection for a denominational commission on world hunger, and on another occasion to serve on a committee considering future directions in seminary education. He impressed some of the professors on the committee, and was invited to lead a retreat for incoming seminary students. He, too, is beginning to get some recognition in the wider church for his theological insights.

At the congregational level, his undergraduate humanities background is often more useful than much of his theological training. He knows how to draw something pertinent out of classics, recent best sellers, and everything between. His sermons are literate without being pretentious. His congregation appreciates that; the way he preaches would have little appeal to the congregation at Lighthouse. In Springfield and in wider United Church circles he is considered a top-notch preacher.

Our two pastors, in short, are each becoming recognized as outstanding. But the basis for that recognition, as well as the ways it is expressed, is very different.

In his study at Lighthouse, Finney has a well-used library, mostly Bible commentaries, and discussions of topics in Scripture. He has a motto on the wall: "Go ye." When members of his flock see that, they know the reference:

> Go ye into all the world, and preach the gospel to every creature. He that believeth and is baptized shall be saved. (Mark 15:15)

They see that motto as entirely fitting. Commitment to the evangelization of the world is exactly what they want in their pastor, in their church, and in themselves.

Chalmers' study has many more, and more varied, books. A very modern cross hangs on the wall, but no motto. He has a motto he would like to have there, but he is afraid some parishioners would misinterpret it, so he put it on the wall in his bedroom instead. He sees it there every day, and it helps him over the rough spots. It reads:

Comfort the afflicted;
Afflict the comfortable.

For him, but not for all of his people, that sums up a central aspect of his calling.

Even with two good churches, each doing its own thing relatively well, however, there are points on which I cannot offer favorable judgement.

A polemic strand runs through much of Pastor Finney's preaching. It is aimed at "modernists," "liberals," "social gospelites," or something of that kind. He doesn't stoop to terms like "Christ-hating" or "commie-loving," labels that some of his classmates use rather freely; those he recognizes as unfair.

"Modernists," Finney had drummed into him at Bible school, reject the authority of the Bible, and so make the Gospel of no effect. They *must* reject it because they do not speak of it as "inerrant." They do not preach Bible doctrines like "substitutionary blood atonement." They reject the blessed hope of Christ's quick return in the clouds to rapture the saints. Their social activism is a kind of works-righteousness...

Many fellow evangelicals consider Finney's position extreme; some see in it relics of a former age. It is certainly not representative of evangelicalism as a whole. But for him it is foundational.

If anyone were to put together specifications for a "modernist" from the preaching at Lighthouse, one would have a hard time finding such a creature. The picture was partly inaccurate and partly exaggerated when first painted two or three generations ago. It has been embroidered on as the years have gone by. In the meantime, whatever basis the image ever had has declined in the churches where it is supposed to prevail. It is a straw man.

Chalmers less often mentions "fundamentalists," but his occasional remarks are just as stereotyped. It would be difficult, however, to draw any sort of characterization of "fundamentalists" from his remarks in sermons. The fact is, he has little idea, right or wrong, of what a "fundamentalist" is, or how one thinks. His seminary courses told him nearly nothing about fundamentalism or any related movements. He picked up a few random comments by professors, fellow students, and friends in the pastorate. He reads an occasional newspaper story. His perception of fundamentalists is fragmentary, confused, and mostly inaccurate. You can't call it a straw man, however—it is just a heap of straw waiting to be formed. That does not prevent him from being frightened by some of the social and political implications of "fundamentalism."

Pastor Finney has rarely talked at any depth with the Rev. Chalmers. On these occasions he has been surprised to find that his stereotypes do not completely match reality. Chalmers seems to be correct on some points on which he ought to be in deep heresy. Other points, though, confirm the stereotypes. Chalmers is obviously unaccustomed to words like "substitutionary," and uncomfortable with old songs like this:

> There is a fountain filled with blood
> Drawn from Immanuel's veins;
> And sinners plunged beneath that flood,
> Lose all their guilty stains.

One of the members from Lighthouse heard Chalmers speak once. Chalmers quoted both Harry Emerson Fosdick and William Golding—and used both to make a quite evangelical point. As expected, Chalmers defended the public schools on the use of books like *Lolita*. But he also took a stand for stronger moral education. That was puzzling; "modernists" were supposed to be against moral education in the schools.

His rare contacts with Finney have left Chalmers puzzled too. Finney is generally suspicious of the public schools, as expected. But he did not support a campaign to remove a teacher who was suspected—but never proved—to be pro-communist. Finney is, predictably, anti-abortion, but not from a rigid moralism. His stand comes from a deep pastoral concern.

Chalmers catches a glimpse of Finney some Mondays at the curling rink. Anybody who curls can't be all bad. He's been thinking that they ought to get together for curling sometime, but he just has never gotten around to asking him. He's not quite sure how to do it.

While there are real differences, many of the disagreements are misunderstandings of each other's language. Their religious vocabularies just don't match. Other differences seem to arise simply from ignorance and from stubborn stereotypes. And each is a little hesitant about how to approach the other.

The name "Lighthouse Bible Church" hints at one side of the second problem. It seems to claim that the church honors the Bible, whereas some other churches do not. In fact, you can hear the members state that "*We* preach the Gospel uncompromised."

This sort of boastful biblicism Finney learned in Bible school and found waiting for him at Lighthouse, the legacy of former pastors of similar training. He emphatically defines faithfulness to the Bible in terms of "inerrancy"—total freedom from error of any sort. He considers this to be explicitly taught in the Bible itself. He insists that biblical "inerrancy" is in historic continuity with Luther's *sola scriptura* and with orthodoxy through the ages. He cannot imagine any other statement about the Bible as being anything other than a flat rejection of its authority.

Finney is on good terms with Rev. Judson Campbell, pastor at Calvary Baptist Church. Campbell is equally emphatic in upholding "inerrancy," and they are broadly in agreement on most other points of doctrine. Yet they do have some disagreements. An outsider might consider their differences trivial, but, for both, small details of doctrine are more important than outsiders appreciate. For example, one holds that the Rapture will occur before the Tribulation, and the other after. Each is a little puzzled at the other's interpretation, since each feels that the Bible basis is entirely clear and the interpretation certain.

> For the Lord himself shall descend from heaven with a shout, with the voice of the archangel, and with the trump of God: and the dead in Christ will rise first: then we which are alive and remain shall be caught up together with them in the clouds to meet the Lord in the air: and so shall we ever be with the Lord. (1 Thessalonians 4:16–17)

Chalmers is secretary of Springfield's ministerial association. Most of the ministers in town participate, but neither Finney nor Campbell do, though they have been invited regularly and cordially. The association has been very active since Rev. Sharon McLeod of Knox Presbyterian Church took the chair. They have organized a joint marriage counseling program, coordinated visiting at the hospital, and operated a small interchurch booth at the county fair.

A few ministers meet every Monday to work together on the lectionary passages for the following Sunday. Sharon McLeod often leads off by asking, "What is this passage saying to me, here and now?" and then, "How can I bring that to life for the congregation?" It is not exactly the same question Wesley Chalmers asks, but it leads her in the same direction.

Another regular participant is Rev. Alistair Smith of St. James' Lutheran Church. Chalmers and Smith find it almost impossible to agree on any definition of the authority of the Bible. Smith can quote verbatim the paragraphs on the Scriptures in Luther's Catechism and the Augsburg Confession (in an English translation!), and give a detailed argument in support of each point. Chalmers can at best roughly summarize his own church's official pronouncements on the Bible; they are not by any means the starting place for his thinking in the matter. Yet each finds the discussion with another who comes from a different theological tradition both stimulating and helpful.

But all in the group give a preeminent place to the Bible in their preaching, and they all endeavor, first of all, to hear what the Scripture says. That is enough, they find, to make their discussion faithful and fruitful, whatever differences they may have.

C halmers and his people hear, at times, bits of the sort of doctrinaire biblicism preached at Lighthouse. They find it, especially in the form it takes on radio and television, at best unattractive and at worst repulsive.

Yet every Sunday they hear the Bible read, and it often speaks to their hearts. They hear preaching that helps them through the rough times, and they know it is based on the Bible. They are not able to say just why, but they feel very strongly that the Bible is in some way foundational.

The members at Central are deeply ambivalent about the Bible. A few try to square it by saying that they are for the Bible but against biblicism, or something like that. But that is no real answer. If you ask them point blank about the authority of the Bible, they have little to say. They are unhappy with "inerrancy," as they hear it applied, say, to the story of creation in Genesis. They try to avoid thinking at all deeply about this matter, and have no ready explanation of where they stand on this chapter or any other controversial passages. The doctrinaire claims that they occasionally hear have made them leery of saying anything very specific about the Bible.

Chalmers, himself, can give a somewhat better answer, but his explanation is larded with theological jargon: "demythologization," "deuteronomistic reformulation," "redaction"... Even the best informed members at Central get lost after about the first few words. Since the United churches give the Bible a central place in both their work and their worship, you might expect them to have a widely known, reasoned statement about biblical authority in language intelligible to ordinary members. Then they too could confidently claim to be biblical— at least as biblical as churches like Lighthouse. But no; unwittingly, they have conceded the field. Lighthouse can go on claiming exclusive possession without challenge from Central, and to reap the benefits of that distinction in a society that has a vague, misshapen, limited, but still vigorous allegiance to the Bible.

MOLDING MINISTERS

The signboard on the lawn in front of Central United Church reads: "The Rev. Wesley Chalmers, B.A., M.Div." The one beside the door at Lighthouse Bible Church reads "Pastor: G. Whitefield Finney." Those two lines reveal a great deal about the two churches, their expectations for their ministers, and the face they present to the public.

Occasionally when he sees that sign, Chalmers wishes that it might be different. He would like to trim off the frills and make it just "Pastor: Wesley Chalmers." He has never risked the minor confrontation that would result. Those "frills" are important to the members of Central; proper qualifications and the corresponding titles for their minister are part of their image of their church.

Finney sometimes wishes he too might have an M.Div. It would give him some better standing in the wider community. It is never more than a fleeting thought, however, because he knows that the price of such a degree would be exposure to infidelity. The members of his church all call him "Brother Finney," on a par with "Brother Elliott" or "Sister Pierce" or any of the other members. He likes that; it keeps him closer to his people.

You could dismiss all this as mere snobbishness and reverse snobbery. "Master of Divinity" is a recognized degree, presuming high academic standards. "Bachelor of Theology" was created by a group of schools with lower entrance requirements to mimic the M.Div, or, rather, its predecessor the Bachelor of Divinity. Though the schools that grant it have improved their standards tremendously, they remain outside the establishment, and the "Th.B." is rarely recognized in academic circles. Yet there is less difference in standards between Finney's Th.B. and Chalmers' M.Div. than many like to think.

Of course, Chalmers has the B.A. also, and Finney does not. A good B.A. gives some breadth that is hard to get otherwise. But some B.A.s are much better than others, and those initials cannot of themselves guarantee anything about the holder.

Yet there is a significant difference in the educational formation of our two ministers. I call it "continuity" versus "disjointedness." The terms aren't very good, but what they signify is crucial.

B oth ministers came from "Christian" families in small towns where the neighbors were largely "Christian" also. That meant that there were certain standards generally adhered to—a "biblical" morality that pervaded secular society.

The Chalmers family never played cards on Sunday; the Finneys never at any time. In neither community would anyone mow the lawn, hang out laundry, or wash the car on Sunday. There was no temptation to go to any commercial entertainment on "the Sabbath"—movie theatres were closed. There wasn't much else at any time, except when the circus came through in the summer, or when the county fair was held in the early fall. And these never operated on Sunday, anyway.

Families might have serious problems, but divorce was not commonly seen as a way out. If divorce should happen, the people concerned generally moved to some other community. So appearances were kept up.

Yet it was not all appearances. There was a fairly high ethical level in business dealings in both towns, and the communities functioned fairly well. They were rooted in the better aspects of Christendom.

A mos Finney, Whitefield Finney's uncle, had been a blacksmith. As that business declined, he came to be a general handyman, fixing whatever needed fixing, doing a bit of rough carpentry, plowing gardens in the spring time, pruning fruit trees, etc. This gave him no great standing in his town. Still he was respected as an honest, if slightly eccentric, workman. He read little but the Bible, but he had read that through and through many times over. In his own way he knew it thoroughly. He could call out of his memory hundreds of verses whenever occasion demanded. He felt a call to preach, and gathered a little flock together. His preaching consisted largely of stringing together Bible verses. It was always delivered without notes—"as the Spirit gives utterance."

He found an abandoned stable, and by his own labor fixed it up, painted a sign on the front that said "Jesus Saves" and called it "Love One Another Tabernacle." Few of the prominent citizens

of Middlefield ever went to that part of town, and the community as a whole was almost completely unaware of its existence.

In the little company was Amos' brother, Joel, who became the deacon when they organized. Joel and his young family, including little Whitey, were there every Sunday morning and every Sunday evening, and every Wednesday for prayer meetings, and whenever there was anything special. Love One Another Tabernacle was a part of their life as essential and unvarying as meals and sleep. When Finney looks back on his childhood, he suspects that the warm sense of unfeigned fellowship kept the group together and attracted new members, at least as much as his uncle's preaching.

Love One Another Tabernacle continued to grow. While Whitey was still a young boy the congregation bought a nearby lot, and started

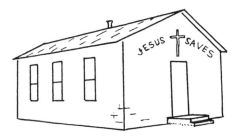 putting up a cement-block building. His earliest memories of church were of services in that still unfinished building with its backless home-made benches and bare light bulbs hanging from the roof trusses. The singing was loud and joyful—and generally a little off key, as they had neither piano nor skilled song leader. But his father, Deacon Joel Finney, did his best to lead the music, loudly and joyfully.

His uncle, preaching behind the small table that served as a pulpit, was, if anything, louder. He was joyful too, as he told of the "precious blood of Jesus that washed away my sin, and can wash away yours, brother." Or of the day soon to come when Jesus would return, "and you know, brothers and sisters, if he comes on a Sunday, right here to Middlefield, where he will come looking for his people? Well, I can tell you, it won't be to those churches on Main Street, but it will be right here on Railroad Street to this poor little house that we have put up for his Glory. And we will be ready to receive Him, Hallelujah! And why will he come here? Because he knows we love him!" And the people would answer "Yes, Lord!" and you could tell they really meant it.

By the time Whitey was in high school, Love One Another Tabernacle had installed wallboard, a ceiling with acoustic tile, nice light fixtures and hardwood pews. The place looked like a church. Yet Brother Amos preached the same message, with the same style of delivery, and in the same folksy language.

A t first Sister Finney—Whitey's Aunt Imogene—taught all the children. As the congregation grew they divided the classes and recruited more teachers. They used the International Uniform Lesson series, with quarterlies from a good "sound" (and inexpensive) publishing house. They supplemented that with a good deal of memorization: the books of the Bible in order (they had contests to see who could find passages fastest), the Ten Commandments, and a string of key verses, starting with John 3:16.

After Sunday School, they all stayed for church, and listened to Brother Amos preach for an hour or so. They returned again in the evening. They heard those verses they knew over and over, and a lot of others. Every verse began to take on meaning for them all. The meanings all hung on the "saving Blood" and the "soon Return" as taught in "His infallible Word."

The hymns they sang were full of those same verbal symbols. One of their favorites was:

> What can wash away my sin?
>   Nothing but the Blood of Jesus;
> What can make me whole again?
>   Nothing but the Blood of Jesus.

> Oh! Precious is the flow
>   That makes me white as snow;
> No other fount I know,
>   Nothing but the Blood of Jesus.

> This is all my hope and peace—
>   Nothing but the Blood of Jesus;
> This is all my righteousness—
>   Nothing but the Blood of Jesus.

Where a United Church preacher might speak of "the incarnation," "the ministry of Jesus," or "the death and resurrection of Christ," Finney and his congregation would gather all these ideas together and speak of "the Blood."

A s a high-school junior, Whitey began to teach a class of younger boys. He fit right into the pattern: read the lesson, comment on it verse by verse (the quarterlies gave a lot of useful hints), check the memory lessons, then have a little Bible contest—perhaps, who can quote the largest number of verses with the word "blood" in them?

None of the Sunday School teachers had the same extensive command of the Bible that Brother Amos had. But they all had exactly the same attitudes toward the Bible, and they all knew exactly what it taught on all the major points of doctrine. Sunday School fit right in with church, and vice versa.

W esley Chalmers was brought up in a very similar town. His father was a lawyer, practising in the county court and having to make occasional trips to other nearby towns or to the city. He was also a pillar of Trinity United Church, generally recognized as *the* church of Barnesborough.

The Chalmers family was always there—except during their vacation at the lake and at Christmas, when they visited one or the other of the grandparent families elsewhere. They always sat in the second pew on the left. They always greeted their neighbors cordially. The pharmacist and his family sat in the other end of the same pew. One of the doctors sat right behind them, and the superintendent of schools across the aisle. Mr. Chalmers would shake hands with many of the other pillars as he came in or went out. It was all very proper and formal.

Through their elementary school days, Wes and his sister listened desultorily to the singing, squirmed a bit during the prayer, perked up a bit for the children's story, and then scurried out during the second hymn to the Sunday School.

Trinity's Sunday School was much like the one at Love One Another Tabernacle. Reginald Scott was the superintendent, and seemed always to have been. Mr. Scott ran the Sunday School with a corps of devoted teachers, most of them well past middle age. Every few years, the church board tried, cautiously, to suggest some changes, but got nowhere. The ministers, who came and went every four to six years, all wished for some updating of curriculum and methods. But hints had no effect, and Mr. Scott and his teachers were rooted immovably.

Mr. Scott would not have thought of himself as a conservative. He would tell anyone who would listen that he was always open to new ideas, if they seemed good. But none of the new ideas ever did. So the Sunday School used the same International Uniform Lessons that Love One Another Tabernacle did. Almost every minister cautiously suggested some other publisher, but Mr. Scott concluded each time that David C. Cook had better helps for "my" teachers, and that ended the matter. The one exception was a minister who brashly pushed a denominational curriculum that was getting rave reviews from Christian education directors across the church. Reginald Scott looked at it and concluded:
a) it would be too hard to teach,
b) it assumed too adult capabilities of the children,
c) it wasn't biblical enough,
d) he had his doubts about the qualifications of anybody who would write that sort of stuff or suggest its adoption.

There was a change of ministers within the year.

The classes read the lessons, the teachers commented verse by verse—or rather, they tried to get the children to comment by asking leading questions. They assigned memory passages—the Ten Commandments, the Beatitudes, and 1 Corinthians 13 were the core—in addition to the memory verses suggested in the quarterlies. They soft-pedalled those passages about blood and said as little as they could about Revelation, and they had a nice wall map to trace out Paul's journeys. But it was otherwise only a more polished version of the teaching at Love One Another Tabernacle.

However, the Bible teaching in the United Church Sunday School wasn't backed up by anything like Amos Finney's preaching, so the children learned much less and retained it a shorter time. But in a few families, like the Chalmers, the parents supported the teaching by their own efforts. Young Wes came out of Sunday School with a number of passages stored in memory, a fair acquaintance with a range of Bible stories, and a moralizing interpretation of many of the texts.

When he got to high school, Wes no longer left for Sunday School in the middle of the service. It took a while to get onto what was going on as he sat through the sermons. Fortunately, the minister at that time was a skillful preacher who could make a message come alive, even for youth. Wes began to see, faintly at first, a different side of the faith.

Looking back after 15 years in the pastoral ministry, Chalmers now understands what puzzled him as a boy. There was a deep intellectual division within Trinity United Church: the lay-run Sunday School totally out of tune with the minister-run worship service.

This was the first bit of "disjointedness" in Wesley Chalmers' preparation. As he was to find out, it was also the experience of most of his fellow ministers.

University took Wes away from home for the first time, and into a very different environment. It was not just the much bigger society—the university had more faculty than Barnesborough had people—it was also much more secular. Most of his Arts professors acted as if religion simply didn't exist; a few made occasional pointed jabs at the church and at religious folk generally. Some of his classmates took their new-found freedom as an occasion to rebel against the religion of their parents. Wes's new environment was also more pluralistic. For the first time, he met Jews, both pious and secular, and he met students from non-Christian countries who took Muslim or Hindu ideas as expected features of the environment, just as he had been raised to expect "Christian" ideas all around him.

Somehow he found his way into the Campus United Church Fellowship. That was almost as strange for him as the secularism or the pluralism. The Fellowship's central concern seemed to be with the great social issues of the day, and the tendency was definitely anti-establishment. He liked what he found and became an active member and, in his third year, an officer. He wrote home that he was attending the Campus United Church Fellowship, and that pleased his family. He thought it best to be selective in reporting just what they did.

The Fellowship members didn't just talk about issues. They set out to do something about them too. Wes found himself working with a group of underprivileged grade-school boys, coaching them in basketball, tutoring them, helping them find themselves. That started him thinking about ministry.

The next time he was home, he went to talk with the new minister at Trinity, and confided in him. He detected a bit of wistfulness in the pastor's voice; the pastor knew about those programs and thought they were great. And, yes, the ministry might give opportunity for continuing service of that sort. The minister said Trinity Church would probably stand behind Wes if he did make that decision.

That Sunday clinched it. The sermon was based on the prophecy of Amos. Just as Amos had done, the new minister played on all the congregation's prejudices only to turn them back against themselves in the end, subtly but surely. Wes wanted to applaud, but you don't do that in United churches. He wondered if the message had gotten across, and he imagined the pastor wondering too. He decided he would like to do things like that himself.

Perhaps that sort of preaching had been there all along, but he had never been consciously aware of it. When he thought back, as a matter of fact, yes, it had been. He was experiencing another bit of that United Church disjointedness. It involved a kind of balancing act, playing off popular biblicism against social justice, all very low key. The Fellowship had sensitized him; many of the other members didn't notice anything.

Young Whitey worked for a year after high school selling fertilizer and farm chemicals. When Aunt Imogene had to give up as superintendent at Love One Another Tabernacle, he took over that responsibility. He even filled in one Sunday when his uncle Amos had flu. That was a little scary, but almost twenty years of listening had implanted the patterns rather thoroughly. After a hesitant start, he found that one verse suggested another, and he went on "opening the Word" pretty much the way his uncle did. It was pretty good for a first attempt. Everybody was proud of him.

The combination of his work and his church started him thinking about the ministry. One Wednesday night when it was time for testimonies, Sister Catherine testified about how much it had meant to her when she finally gave up and agreed to follow Jesus in just everything. She had given that same testimony, pretty much word for word, for years. This time it did something new for Whitey. When she sat down, Whitey got up and told the people that he had heard a call to preach. He confessed that he had been fighting against it; but the Lord had just now prevailed. That night while Sister Catherine was testifying, he had yielded too. Then Sister Catherine got up and testified how she had always prayed for Whitey since he was a little tike in her primary class, and now her prayer had been answered, Praise the Lord. They all prayed for Whitey like they had done when he "came through" at the revival nine years before. They thanked God for picking one from their little number for the Lord's special ministry.

The next September, Love One Another Tabernacle, with great rejoicing, sent Whitey off to Bible School, and agreed to help with his expenses. Those expenses were a lot less than Chalmers was paying in the university, but it was still a heavy burden on the congregation at Love One Another Tabernacle. They accepted it gladly; it was their response to God's goodness to them, and they were mighty proud of "our boy."

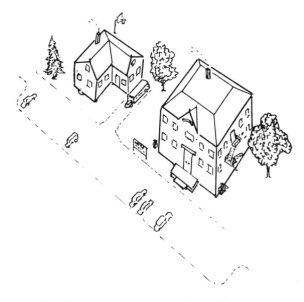

B eing away from home for the first time was as difficult for Whitey as it was for Wes Chalmers. But he was in a small group of people. There were only about sixty students. All had much the same sort of background; all had the same convictions and purposes; all had a definite call first into the faith and then into full-time service; and all had home churches standing behind them. There were four paid faculty members; they all shared that same background too. It was as supportive an environment as one could ask. In many ways it was like Love One Another Tabernacle at its best.

Bible School could be compared to a five-day Sunday School. Teaching was pretty much as Whitey had known it at Love One Another

Tabernacle, but more intensive and much deeper. In four years, his class went through most of the Bible, examining it verse by verse. They memorized passages. They memorized the outlines of each book. They memorized the "key verses" for each doctrinal point.

At the graduation ceremony, the president explained how much he regretted that they couldn't cover the whole Bible in four years, but "the Bible is a wondrous book, full of truth to extend through a lifetime of Bible study and more." Then he fell back on the confidence that his little school had given the thirteen graduates the basis for a lifetime of Bible study.

Bible School was in direct continuity with the students' education in their home churches. Of course, the teachers were better prepared than the Sunday School teachers back home. They knew the Bible even more thoroughly than Brother Amos. They also had four advantages over him.

- First, they had all had better preparation. None had had to work their understanding of Bible out on their own.
- Second, they had a library with a collection of sound books.
- Third, they had colleagues with whom to discuss problems of interpretation.
- Fourth, they didn't have to mow lawns and do odd jobs eight hours a day to live. The Bible School paid them a modest salary, so they could put full time into study and teaching.

Whitey benefited from the deeper and broader knowledge of his teachers. He also benefited directly from some of the resources that had made his teachers what they were. The school library, though not half as big as the library in his high school, was 90% on the Bible, and filled with riches he had never dreamed of. Before he got there, Whitey had never seen anything more elaborate than the little concordance bound in the back of his Bible. He had found that useful, even though Uncle Amos felt that it was much better to rely on your own memory. Now there was Strong's *Exhaustive Concordance of the Bible*, one of the biggest, heaviest books he had ever seen, though printed in very small type. He no longer had to wonder about words like "ephod"; there was a Bible dictionary with a picture.

The faculty taught him how to use the most basic tools. Being of a curious bent, he looked into everything else on his own. He worked out for himself the use of all the tools he could find that the faculty didn't cover. That was all new, but it was only a matter of better tools. Both in class and out of class he used them for the same purpose: Get thoroughly acquainted with the Bible—the King James Version, of course. Store as much of it away in memory as you can. Learn to retrieve what you need when you need it. Interpret it all around Blood, Return, and Inerrancy.

G. Whitefield Finney felt none of the disjointedness that Wesley Chalmers experienced between Sunday School and church, between home community and university, between Trinity Church and the Campus United Church Fellowship. Love One Another Tabernacle and The Word Bible School were in continuity, as would be Lighthouse Bible Church when he got there.

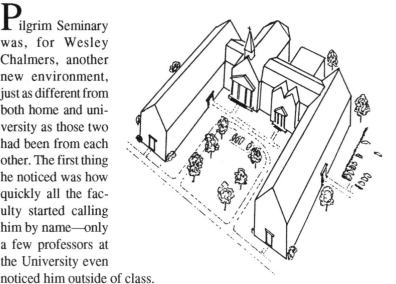

Pilgrim Seminary was, for Wesley Chalmers, another new environment, just as different from both home and university as those two had been from each other. The first thing he noticed was how quickly all the faculty started calling him by name—only a few professors at the University even noticed him outside of class.

The campus was a smaller edition of the university's physical environment. The classrooms looked much the same: blackboards, with a few cryptic inscriptions left over from the previous class, chalk usually down to a couple of very small pieces, a lectern, chairs with awkward arms for note taking. The procedures were much the same: the professor lectured, the students took notes. The first day included the same presentation of the requirements: long reading lists, papers to be written, and in some courses, midterms and a final.

In history Chalmers could make a direct comparison between seminary and university. In his senior B.A. year he had had a course in the history of the classical world. Now he was listening to lectures on the history of the church in approximately the same period. It started just at the close of the "apostolic period"—that, he soon figured out, marked the division of jurisdiction between the New Testament Department and the Church History Department. He had heard nothing in university of a major division point at this time.

The dates "Common Era" in university and "Anno Domini" here could be equated. If the dates were deleted from each account, he concluded, it would become impossible to match up anything until the time of Constantine. Even the general social background to the events seemed out of touch. The seminary professor had a lot to say about Hellenistic Judaism, for example, but the university course had never mentioned anything of the kind.

The Introduction to Old Testament course puzzled Chalmers most, and occasionally shocked him. Professor Rufus Bartram used no notes in his lecture, just a Hebrew "Tanach"—it took the students some time to figure out that that was simply a Hebrew Bible, with the books in the Jewish arrangement. He didn't read it to the class, but he always translated on the fly; so the English came out slightly different if he returned to comment on a verse a second time. Though he was one of the older members of the faculty, nearing retirement, he delighted in injecting very current slang into his interpretations. He often set them in sharp relief to the fairly pompous wordings of the Revised Standard Version that Chalmers carried to class.

When students asked Professor Bartram what translation he preferred them to use, they detected a slight contempt for all English translations. He took the question as an opportunity to plug Hebrew—an elective subject at Pilgrim, as in most seminaries.

The course had started out with a discussion of J, E, P, and later brought in D and H, interwoven documents that had been skillfully brought together to make the text "we know," but not skillfully enough that modern scholars could not tease them apart again. To make his points, Bartram emphasized differences between one passage and another, and of course, his *ad hoc* translation into English gave him opportunity to sharpen these differences a little. He started right out with Genesis 1 and 2, familiar passages to those who, like Chalmers, had a strong Sunday School background. He avoided any moralizing—Chalmers couldn't help contrasting Reginald Scott talking, at every opportunity, about how giving in to temptations could have dreadful consequences not just for the person but for others, as Eve's had for us all.

Bartram dissected the text. This verse—occasionally this phrase—represented one tradition, and that another. He didn't even bother to discuss whether Moses had had a part in writing Genesis. He talked, instead, about anonymous writers from various places and dates who had produced the documents he labelled J, E, P, H, and D and the editors who had stuck the pieces together.

One Monday, Professor Bartram mentioned, quite casually, something about the World Series game the day before. A student—one with a Sunday School background much like Chalmers'—asked what Bartram felt the Ten Commandments had to say about Sunday games. The reply was, "Nothing at all. First, the Ten Commandments say nothing whatever about baseball. Second, they say nothing whatever about Sunday. Now maybe if it had been a Saturday game..."

That was a shock. Then it came out that the professor had been in the ball park on Sunday to see the game he had mentioned. It was a tense moment for at least one student.

They all learned, much later, that Bartram's second great love was baseball, and his hobby was umpiring in the county league. Bartram had this idea about umpiring. You had to get it out of the minds of managers that they were running the show. Shake 'em up a bit, good and hard, their first game. But he had a reputation as fair and consistent, with an eye for the strike zone that could have qualified him for the big leagues.

He had a similar idea about teaching Old Testament. You start out by disabusing them of a lot of ideas they had picked up in Sunday School. Some of his colleagues called it "shock treatment."

Chalmers thought Professor Bartram looked a little like Reginald Scott. But his approach, though just as brusque, was exactly the opposite. He combined a touch of studied irreverence with a great love of the Old Testament. You got the feeling that his mission in life was to protect the Old Testament from over-pious Sunday School teachers.

Shock treatment wasn't working anymore like it had when Bartram started out as a young assistant professor with a new Ph.D. from Harvard University. At that time, forty years earlier, a majority of the students came to seminary with a fair knowledge of English Bible and a lot of superficial interpretations that set them up for him. Now only a minority knew very much. But he still played the game for what it was worth. And one way or another he did shake up most of them.

In Chalmers' second year at seminary, Old Testament was taught by Professor Zdenka Novakova. The shift of emphasis was dramatic. The younger professor, trained in Europe two decades later than Bartram, took the history-of-religion approach. Her lectures dwelt on parallels between Hebrew religion as reconstructed from the Bible and other religions in the ancient Near East: Sumerian, Assyrian, Egyptian, Canaanite—you name it. At first it seemed to the students that the Old Testament sometimes got lost behind a detailed comparison of the gods Isis and Astarte, or of Babylonian and Canaanite sacrifice. But as the year went on, most came to see how it all contributed to a better understanding not only of the biblical text but of its significance for today.

Bartram was always ready to put in a soft-sell for Hebrew. Novakova's answers to questions commonly included some enticing reference to a paper in the technical literature, coupled with an implicit lament that too few were equipped to read anything important these days. She often listed publications in French and German, and occasionally Latin or Italian. Once in a while she would mention, wistfully, a Czech publication "which, unfortunately, nobody else at Pilgrim is equipped to read."

Wesley Chalmers tried tracking down some of these references. Sometimes they were interesting and informative. The European ones often had an English abstract, presumably intended to give a prospective reader some idea of what the article contained. They helped him pick the ones worth struggling over. Even thought he had read Flaubert in university, he found there were new skills to be learned for reading theological French. Once in a while he found the English abstract so daunting he didn't dare try the paper. But from Professor Novakova's comments and his own efforts, he came to appreciate something of the vast extent of biblical scholarship. For that he has always thanked her, even though he seldom sees any of that literature now; no one else in Springfield misses it.

Chalmers invented a little game in Bartram's class: listening for anything he could imagine Reginald Scott would have understood enough to blow up over. Almost every lecture had something interesting that way. Almost without exception, it would be some minor verbal matter. He was quite sure that his old superintendent would never have gotten the real substantive stuff. It would be just as well. Bartram's subversion of Moses' authorship Scott would have understood, and he would have had a heart attack on the spot. Novakova's finding non-Hebraic roots for everything in the Old Testament would have been much worse. Fortunately, communication between the Seminary and Trinity United Sunday School in Barnesborough was quite tenuous.

Professor Rufus Bartram commuted to seminary from Nazareth Corners, thirty miles out of town. Few of the seminary students even knew where he lived. I was, however, invited out there once to preach an anniversary sermon. They couldn't pay enough to get any big name, but I figured what they offered would pay my 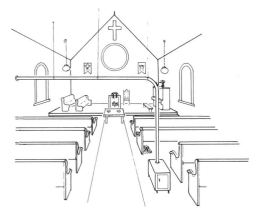 gas, and that the country dinner would be ample reward. It was. I ate with Mrs. Dougal McAllister, who lived across the road from professor Bartram. She told us a lot about their little Nazareth United Church, and she showed me another side of her neighbor. On the campus no one would have thought of calling him anything less formal than "Rufus"; most called him "Professor Bartram"; a few insisted on "Dr. Bartram."

But he was simply "Rufe" to all the local people.

In Mrs. McAllister's own words: "Reverend Aberystwyth is a fine young man and a good preacher and we think a lot of him. But for making the Gospel clear, he don't hold a candle to Rufe. Rufe teaches our Willing Workers' Class. You know, Nazareth is the only United Church in the county that still has an adult class. Every Sunday he gives us something interesting and inspiring, and right down the line with the Bible. Sakes alive! Does that man know his Bible! Gives me something to think about all week as I wash and sweep and cook for Dougal. Nobody in Nazareth Corners would miss Sunday School even if the Trumpet of the Lord blew that morning. Even Sandy Campbell comes— and he's a stiff-backed Presbyterian! We had thirty-five out last Sunday."

Moving back and forth between the seminary classroom and the country church was much like moving between "Professor Rufus Bartram" and "Rufe"—a matter of style rather than basic content. His love for the Bible preserved the integrity of his message while he adjusted his presentation to his hearers.

Chalmers and his classmates sensed the disjointedness of their education, as they alternated every week between field work and campus—between two different intellectual climates. They heard from last year's students about misadventures of starting in full-time ministry and their frustrations with ordination councils, personnel committees, and other church structures. Long before graduation, they felt the system closing in on them, and began to see the administrative hoops they would have to jump through. Only pushed into the background was the tension between Pilgrim Seminary's approach (or approaches) to the Bible and the reality they knew they would face out there—and perhaps in their journey through those hoops as well.

They didn't even need to look that far ahead. The third year students were all enrolled in a course entitled "The Use of the Bible in Teaching and Preaching." It was taught by the pastor of a prestigious local church, a famous pulpit performer. He had a lot of practical experience to share. The students generally liked the course, but it said nothing about J, E, P, Ugarit, or Qumran, and so left still unanswered a lot of their questions about how the Bible they studied in seminary related to the Bible the church reads in its worship.

Had students from The Word Bible School overheard that class, they would have been amazed that it left so much freedom. Their classes not only explicitly laid down rules about how to use the Bible, the classes themselves constituted a model. For that matter, they would be amazed that there could be a course in preaching *followed by* a course in the use of the *Bible* in preaching.

Finney and his classmates went out into their first pastorates with none of the tensions experienced by the seminary students. The churches they went to were all much like the churches they had come from, even when the communities were quite different. Nothing they had learned could not be directly used in teaching and preaching, nothing needed circumspect restatement, little needed even an adjustment in vocabulary. It is only a slight exaggeration to suggest that they could take their class notes unchanged into the pulpit as sermon outlines!

Chalmers and his classmates, going to their first pastorates, saw yet another face of disjointedness. They were not merely going from seminary into a parish, but often going into a strangely different part of the church. One city-bred new graduate found herself serving three small churches where the roads were all gravel, urban amenities largely missing, and local church customs often strange. It was difficult at first both for the people and the new pastor, but she made it, and settled in after a year or so for a good pastorate. Few realize how much the patience and understanding of some small country charges contribute to the education of ministers!

Chalmers' small-town background made it a little easier when he went to a remote mining community, but there was still a wrenching change. The rows of company houses, the constant awareness of mining hazards, and the consuming struggle between management and the union were in sharp contrast with the outward serenity of his home town. Under those circumstances, worship took on a different meaning, and preaching a new challenge: "What is the good news in these passages, for *this* day, *this* place, and *these* people?" Chalmers had some deep thinking to do.

He began to see that the only thing which could hold the United Church together in the face of its diversity and its disjointedness was precisely that good news given to the churches in the Scriptures. He had never thought of the Bible in just that way before.

SPRINGFIELD'S PAST

S pringfield, four or five generations ago, was a busy little town. From the main corner at almost any time of day you could see one or two—maybe even three—spring wagons coming or going, carrying farmers and their wives for shopping or other business. Heavier wagons carried coal from the railway yards to residences, or merchandise to the stores. Occasionally a town carriage would trot proudly by on some errand where either distance or dignity ruled out walking.

The traffic started early. The milk wagons began making their deliveries about five o'clock. Very soon after came a parade of Irish women from the east end, on their way to prepare breakfast and start their daily chores in the more prominent homes of the town. A little later businessmen walked to their stores and offices. The ebb and flow continued in a familiar rhythm until dark, every working day.

Sunday started a little later. It had a different, but even more pronounced, rhythm. Many of the maids had the day off, and others started later, to work only half a day. A little before nine-thirty the sidewalks were filled with families going to Sunday School and church. It seemed like everybody went, morning and evening. In fact, a few families were pretty lax about the evening services.

Henry Withers and his family never went at any time—but he was a little odd, and something of an embarrassment to the community.

F ive churches were commonly counted, and everybody knew all five, and their pecking order (though no one would have described it that way). Each was presided over by a pastor and a group of the most prominent men in the congregation. First Congregational Church topped the list. It had on its Prudential Committee the mayor, the president of the bank, the owner-manager of the barrel factory, the judge, and a retired farmer reputed

to own thousands of acres of very good land.

Then came Knox Presbyterian Church with its Board of Elders, including the leading lawyer, the sheriff, the principal of the high school, and a couple of prominent physicians.

Springfield Methodist Church had on its Official Board the third doctor, the owner of the hardware store, the funeral director, and a couple of retired farmers (not quite as wealthy, but unquestionably well off).

Last was the Calvary Baptist Church; its four deacons were the owner-operator of the livery stable, the foreman at the barrel factory, one of the grocers, and the constable.

All four of those churches thought of themselves—and the others— as "evangelical" churches. They were quite uncertain about the fifth. The sign said:

CHURCH OF THE EPIPHANY
Rector: Canon Archibald Cranmer
Morning Prayer: 11:00 a.m.
Evening Prayer: 7:00 p.m.
Communion: First and Third Sundays, 9:00 a.m.

There were so many things strange about that. "Rector" instead of "Minister." That odd title "Canon." "Morning Prayer" instead of "Service" or "Worship." Communion at a separate time. When asked, Canon Cranmer would patiently explain that in "the old country" churches like Epiphany would be called "Church of England," but that did not fit here. Some people used "Episcopal" and some "Anglican," but really, for him

and his flock, it was just the Church— a branch of the ancient church that had freed itself from the errors of Rome without the excesses of Luther and Calvin. Somehow that didn't satisfy either the ministers or the members of the evangelical churches. Members of the evangelical churches visited Epiphany much less often than they did other churches. Some strange customs made them uncomfortable, to say the least. The Epiphany people knelt for "prayers"—some were read out of those Prayer Books, and some were chanted. In the evangelical churches prayer was always spontaneous; at least, everyone was careful to make it *appear* spontaneous.

At Epiphany the choir and the rector and a couple of other people marched in all dressed in a strange way—"cassock and surplice" they called it. The people even stood for the reading of the Gospel. It was simply not the "simplicity of reformed worship" or "New Testament worship" that the other churches cherished (each in its own special version, of course).

Yet Epiphany's congregation was largely made up of quite respectable people. The wardens were a highly respected businessman and a retired judge. It was right up there in social status with First Congregational and Knox Presbyterian—but it just didn't fit comfortably with the other churches.

M ost people counted only these five churches. Actually, there were two more. St. Patrick's was over in the east end beyond the barrel factory where the Irish all lived. It had a plaster statue ("image" it was commonly called by  the non-Irish people who saw it) of Mary in front, and a cross on the gable, and was thoroughly "popish." No one ever thought of it along with the five proper churches. But it did serve to remind evangelical people, from time to time, that "not everybody in this world believed the Bible," and the exceptions weren't just occasional eccentrics like Henry Withers either.

There was also a little frame building on the south side across the railroad tracks which had a sign "Evangelische Lutherische Jakobi Kirche". It looked quite like a church, and some had heard it called "St. James Lutheran Church"; but if it was why didn't it say so? The Presbyterian pastor noticed that "Jakobi" looked like the Greek for "James" and thought that maybe the rumor was pretty close. The Baptist

deacon who, as a police constable, had to patrol that part of town, wondered, "If they are Christians, how come they don't speak English, like the New Testament church did?"

Whatever the case might be, they weren't counted in with the churches either. Their pastor, Pfarrer [Pastor] Ehrhardt Weissgerber, didn't mind that. He was too busy tending his little flock (who, as recent immigrants, had plenty of problems), and teaching the children German and catechism after school, and pondering Lutheran theology. He was far too busy to worry about those other churches with their strange ways; they would probably turn out to be tainted with Calvinism anyway.

All five of the "proper" church buildings had much in common. Each had a large sanctuary—though the Baptist one was noticeably smaller than the others—over a basement where the Sunday School met.

The Church of the Epiphany was, as might be expected, the most different. There was a chancel with an "altar" (not a "communion table") and seats for the choir, and a pulpit on one side and a lectern on the other. Each of the others had a central pulpit, a good solid structure—except in the Baptist church, where the pulpit could be moved aside for baptisms to allow a view of the baptistry behind. Each had a communion table in front of the pulpit; the Methodist church had, in addition, an altar rail. The Presbyterian pulpit was a good bit higher than any of the others, to allow for a precentor's desk below it; from this the singing was led.

On each of the pulpits was a Bible, all of them very much alike; if some prankster had gone in one Saturday night and switched them all around, chances are that the switch would have gone unnoticed for several Sundays.

The Presbyterians sang only psalms Sunday morning, and they sang

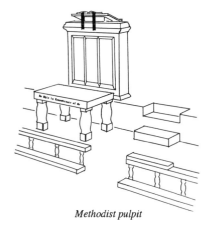

Methodist pulpit

them without accompaniment; that's why they had the precentor to lead them. The other four all sang hymns, though there were some subtle differences in the hymns they sang. And all four had organs—a very elaborate one at First Congregational and a very simple one at Calvary Baptist.

The evening services were much less different. The Presbyterians had recently acquired a piano, which they made as unobtrusive as possible in the morning but played with gusto in the evening. All except Epiphany made some use of the new "gospel songs."

Canon Cranmer's sermons were shorter than the others; they left the impression that he did not consider them the central focus of the service. Elsewhere the preaching was pretty much the same, heavily expository in the morning, and quite evangelistic in the evening. The Congregational and Presbyterian pastors read from manuscripts lying on top of the Bible, and so remained pretty well rooted behind the pulpit. The Methodist and Baptist preachers were not so tied down, and were more exuberant anyway. The Baptist pastor, particu-

Presbyterian pulpit

larly, gave the impression of "winging it." The Presbyterian preached a little longer than the rest, perhaps ten or fifteen minutes longer.

In the past, the four evangelical churches had been a good bit more different. Every time one of them made some small change it brought that church a little closer to a common pattern.

The ministers were highly respected. They all carried heavy civic responsibilities, being expected to participate in appropriate ways in all public functions. One would say the grace at the firemen's picnic; one would lead an opening prayer at the grammar-school graduation, and another would close it with a suitably "nonsectarian" benediction. And so it went.

Canon Cranmer's public prayers had a slightly different flavor. Only the Epiphany members understood the difference: they were largely drawn right out of the Prayer Book. With all the others, if you kept your eyes shut, as proper people all did, you could hardly tell who was praying.

There was a baccalaureate service every year for the high school. It rotated between the five churches. The host pastor welcomed the crowd and opened the service, and the others divided the rest of the service between them. The high school choir sang—an appropriate religious song. The flag from the school auditorium stood at the right front of the sanctuary. Everybody was expected to come, of course. Most did, even Henry Withers, the non-believer, the year his girl graduated. Nobody noticed the absence of the Lutheran and Catholic parents.

The high school was, after the churches and the barrel factory, the most imposing building in town. On the lintel over the front door was carved in large letters, "Ye shall know the truth, and the truth shall make you free." What could be a more appropriate inspiration? The Presbyterian and Congregational ministers knew that that wasn't quite what John 8:32 meant, but they never said anything about it. After all, the imputed meaning was sound enough. And they approved of keeping the Bible in the public attention.

Sunday before election day the Congregational church always had a sermon on "Our Christian Duty as Citizens." Something like that theme would be worked into the sermon in each of the other churches as well, whatever the main topic of the day. The text was usually from the Old Testament, a passage dealing with the nation of Israel as the elect people of God.

Any major patriotic festival inevitably called for attention. The perceived danger was often that the firecrackers, parades, and general festivities would hide from the public the biblical roots of our society and laws. The people had to be reminded of all that. Society was Christian without necessarily being Baptist or Methodist or Congregational or Presbyterian or whatever. It was a disembodied Christianity, quite in the public domain. Its support was a civic reading of the Bible.

That reading was the *de facto* constitution of society. Other than at those annual events, little was said in church services about public affairs. The Sunday Schools, however, played their part. The Old Testament received as much attention as the New. Much of that attention was devoted to the political history of Israel as a model for their society. Romans 13 came around every few years, and Paul was interpreted as a nineteenth-century patriot demanding, in the name of God, all the standard civic virtues.

When a crisis arose, the evangelical churches' reaction was immediate and decisive. One year some of the Irish got up a petition and nominated Sean Monahan for alderman. All the pastors immediately saw it as their duty to remind the people that papism would undercut allegiance to the Bible, undermine public morality, subvert Christian liberties, and generally work havoc in society. Of course, Monahan was not mentioned by name; that would be meddling in politics, which the churches resolutely refused to do.

The mayor consulted his pastor on every issue that had any moral implications—with his superior knowledge of the Bible, the pastor was obviously the expert. On a big question the mayor would talk to all five of the pastors, or even get them together for a meeting. Some moral issues were pressing. "Alcoholism" hadn't been invented yet, but "habitual drunkenness" was familiar, and a continuing concern. There was beer in the south end and Irish whiskey in the east end, and they were often consumed publicly. Only Henry Withers ever asked out loud where all those barrels made in Springfield went to; but he was, as we mentioned, a little eccentric and occasionally a trouble maker! Besides, Henry Withers set a bad example for the youth by his own drinking and his open scorn for all the churches.

Little was said in the church services, in any of the churches, or in the usual interdenominational debates, about the authority of the Bible. It was taken for granted. It was taught in the Sunday Schools, largely by example as biblical passages were discussed. Songs were a favorite medium, and all the churches used:

> Jesus loves me this I know,
> For the Bible tells me so.

Little ones to him belong;
We are weak but he is strong.

There was abundant evidence that all four of the evangelical churches accepted the authority of the Bible. For one thing, every sermon had to be rooted in some text, and every point made had to be supported by a text—preferably a handful of them. In any debate about religion or morality, speakers made points by bringing forth an appropriate text or two. No text could be countered merely by bringing a differing text. Rather, each of the opponent's offerings had to be shown to be either misinterpreted or misapplied. That could lead to forceful debate about the *interpretation* of a verse, but never about its *authority*.

Any action taken by any one of the churches had to be in accordance with the Bible, as that church read it. So did any public decision on a matter of morality—based on a consensus of all recognized churches. Most people felt that the moral teaching of the Bible was pretty clear anyway; it was only some fine doctrinal points that anyone could misinterpret (that is, come out with some other result than what seemed obvious to the speaker).

A lthough the preaching was all much alike, there were somewhat greater differences in official doctrines. That fact gave ample opportunity for debate. The evangelical churches might argue over infant baptism. Or over predestination (some Methodists liked to say that meant "what will be will be even if it ain't"). Often the debate was over perseverance of the saints (that was what the Presbyterians called it; the Baptists preferred "once saved, always saved"). All but the Methodists professed to abhor Wesleyan perfectionism or holiness, and would combat it at any opportunity. Yet they all sang Charles Wesley's *Love divine, all loves excelling*, unaware of its perfectionist message.

S ince the authority of the Scripture was the keystone of the rules under which debate was conducted, it was seldom questioned directly. Occasionally, if debate on some other topic had taken a strange twist, some argument might have to be bolstered by making very explicit not so much that the Bible had authority, but just *how* it had authority. Then, once the question of authority had emerged, each church had its characteristic approach.

The Presbyterians cited their catechism. Many of them had memorized a great deal of it in childhood, and the first few answers stuck most vividly in their memory:

Question 1. What is the chief end of man?
Answer. Man's chief end is to glorify God, and to enjoy him forever.
Question 2. What rule hath God given to direct us how we may glorify and enjoy him?
Answer. The Word of God, which is contained in the Scriptures of the Old and New Testaments, is the only rule to direct us how we may glorify and enjoy him.
Question 3. What do the Scriptures principally teach?
Answer. The Scriptures principally teach what man is to believe concerning God, and what duty God requires of man.

To non-Presbyterians, that seemed a little tangential to the main issue, but there was nothing fundamentally wrong with it. Learned Presbyterians could also cite the Westminster Confession. This had ten long paragraphs going into a great deal more detail, including phrases like "the infallible truth and divine authority thereof" and "given by inspiration of God, to be the rule of faith and life."

The Methodist preacher quoted the Articles of Religion, the statement of faith of the Methodist denomination:

The Holy Scriptures contain all things necessary to salvation; so that whatsoever is not read therein, nor may be proved thereby, is not to be required of any man, that it should be believed as an article of faith, or be thought requisite or necessary to salvation.

Lay Methodists simply dismissed any question about the authority of the Bible as not requiring formal argument. Besides, the Presbyterian statements made it too much a matter of the mind, whereas real religion was a matter of the heart. They knew the Bible was true because it spoke to their hearts, and that was all that was necessary.

The Baptists would say that they rejected creeds and catechisms and articles of religion and all those man-made aberrations, and they would remind their hearers of the penalty of adding to, or subtracting from, the Word of God by quoting the Bible directly:

For I testify unto every man that heareth the words of the prophecy of this book, If any man shall add unto these things, God shall add unto him the plagues that are written in this book: And if any man shall take away from the words of the book of this prophecy, God shall take away his part out of the book of life, and out of the holy city... (Revelation 22:18–19)

The Scripture itself was enough, they said, because it was inspired by God, as Paul said:

All scripture is given by inspiration of God, and is profitable for doctrine, for reproof, for correction, for instruction in righteousness (2 Timothy 3:16)

The Congregationalists pointed out that their church was founded on a covenant with Jesus Christ and with each other. The Bible was what taught them of Christ and of the mind of Christ. So the Bible was just as foundational to them as to any others, but they didn't see any need of getting into any sort of hair splitting about it. But if anyone insisted on a succinct statement, they might quote the following *description*. (Congregationalists were as leery as Baptists about creeds, but there could be no harm in *describing* what they all shared.):

They [the Congregational churches] agree in belief that the Holy Scriptures are the sufficient and only infallible rule of religious faith and practice...

That Congregational description, actually, described them all pretty well.

Debate, when it occurred, quickly switched from the authority of the Bible to how the authoritative Bible was to be used and how that authority was to be applied. Everybody agreed, basically, that the Bible had the answers. The problem, they further agreed, was to interpret it properly. There were many false interpretations. Denominational differences generally boiled down to what interpretations each judged correct and what erroneous.

The Presbyterians and Congregationalists were willing, by and large, to trust their ministers as interpreters. Their ministers were trained for that, and well trained too.

The Methodists and Baptists were cautious; they didn't wish to seem impolite, but they had a fundamental mistrust of academic approaches to religion, and of the elitism of college-educated ministers, who too easily lost touch with common folk. They liked to remind folks that in the early church not many wealthy and not many learned people had been called. Jesus had relied on fishermen, and the like, and he never went through college.

These Springfield churches were caught up in what later came to be called "classical evangelicalism," or "the evangelical consensus," or something like that. Out of this emerged the similarities and the differences between Central and Lighthouse, many years later.

Classical evangelicalism was a consensus around two great principles: the authority—religious, moral, and civil—of the Bible; and the distinction between the saved and the unsaved, between evangelizers and evangelizees. The Bible recorded a Scripture-believing church as a pattern for them. They saw the Reformation as a return to the Scripture from a Roman church that had substituted another non-biblical authority. It was, therefore, also a return to the New Testament pattern for the church. They were duty-bound to call all who had strayed from that pattern back to the Bible.

In actual operation, classical evangelicalism was only a partial consensus. In Springfield, Epiphany was only marginally involved. A major part of the reason was the Prayer Book. It put liturgy at the center, not preaching.

If challenged about this, Canon Cranmer would have responded in a way parallel to any Presbyterian response: The Prayer Book is based on the Bible, conformed to the Bible, and incorporates a great deal of Bible. Its authority is derived from Scripture in the same way as Presbyterians claimed for the Westminster Confession.

There was a big difference, however. At Epiphany the Prayer Book was in constant use by the *people*. At Knox Presbyterian the Catechism was in use only in the Christian education program; the Westminster Confession was only occasionally mentioned in the sermons. The Presbyterian people may have had as much direct exposure to the Bible; but at Epiphany there was more participation in Bible-based liturgy.

If The Church of the Epiphany was marginally in the evangelical consensus, St. Patrick's and Evangelische Lutherische Jakobi Kirche stood completely outside. On the one hand, this evangelicalism was a strictly North American phenomenon, rooted in English-speaking society and entangled in its politics. New arrivals from the continent, German, Scandinavian, Dutch, or whatever, even if they were staunchly Protestant, could have no part in this evangelical consensus until they first learned

English, and then accepted North American church ways. So the German Lutherans were automatically excluded.

On the other hand, the evangelical consensus was centered in a Protestantism that could not forget the polarization of the Reformation. Rome was the ultimate enemy. St. Patrick's was the enemy within the gates.

Rome would remain the enemy until some other enemy could take its place. That was at least half a century down the road. For some the new enemy would be "modernism"; for others "fundamentalism."

With changing times, classical evangelicalism had to change. It could go two ways. One was a hardening of its principles, and the other a softening of them. Important parts of those two processes happened at the grassroots. We can see them—and the resulting deep division—right in Springfield.

Lighthouse Bible Church today stands in the evangelical heritage through a line that made its biblicism more rigid, and that drew more tightly the line between the saved and the unsaved. Central United Church stands in the same evangelical heritage, but through a line that made its biblicism more flexible, and that drew the line around itself less sharply.

NEW ALIGNMENTS

A constant succession of small changes brought Springfield to what I have just described. A continuing succession of small changes—some seeming at the time to be inconsequential—would take it further. Anyone who knows Springfield today can hardly believe that all the changes were small, but they were. The cumulative result was not.

O nly a few of the old businesses survive, and those are so changed as to be almost unrecognizable. New businesses have sprung up. The barrel factory has long been closed, and is now almost forgotten. A highly automated producer of paper clips, safety pins, and other small wire-based objects has taken its place as the chief employer.

Spring wagons and carriages have given way to automobiles. The businessmen no longer walk to work; they drive. There are business-women now, and they drive too. Parking has supplanted moral concerns as the recurrent, insolvable preoccupation for the town council.

Families too no longer walk to church; they drive. So parking has become a central problem for the churches also. Central United met that challenge by buying two fine old homes right behind the church and clearing them to make an ample parking lot. Calvary Baptist took a different route, selling their building and erecting a new one on a five acre lot on the edge of town. That gave the new Lighthouse Bible Church their chance, and they moved out of their rented storefront into the old Baptist building.

Meanwhile, Central United, no longer content with holding Sunday School in the basement, had put on a large, very modern addition. A highly skilled architect did a marvelous job of blending it in with the old building. This addition, more than anything else, made Lighthouse look "modest" by comparison. Of course, the old Baptist building had always been a bit smaller and plainer than the others. The Lighthouse Bible Church people now dream of the day they can move out, too, and solve both the parking problem and the space problem that they inherited.

After thirty years as the beloved priest at St. Patrick's, Fr. Michael Ryan died. The bishop sent them Fr. Rocco Mangione. There were anguished appeals to the bishop. However, Fr. Mangione was a genial and flexible man. In his first parish, he had learned to play polka music like an expert—he would have gotten out on the dance floor and learned to polka too, but priests didn't do that. So within a few years he could sing "When Irish eyes are smiling" with the best of them. The people slowly but surely took him in as one of themselves. Some of the older people continued to wish for a more conventional pastor, but the young people were all for Mangione.

Pavel Dumbrowski came to Springfield to set up a new plastic-bag factory. His family started attending St. Patrick's, but for many years felt like outsiders. His daughter, Ivana grew up there and graduated from Springfield High School. A year later she married Patrick Donohue. Each family had its ideas—national traditions, perhaps—of how in-laws behaved. It took a couple of years to get that all sorted out and everything functioning smoothly, but it happened. There were others. Gradually, St. Patrick's changed from an Irish Catholic parish to a simply Catholic one. Fr. Mangione led the way, and helped make it one of the liveliest parishes in the diocese.

The big strain came with Vatican II. The altar was moved out from the wall, and the mass began to be said in English. It was all very strange. But, "if the Holy Father says so, we'll do it." Actually, it wasn't quite that way, but that was close enough to get St. Patrick's moving in the new direction.

Some of the Irish young people started going off to university. A few of them came back. Michael Reiley became a prominent lawyer in town. Then his son, David, returned from law school to join his father's firm. A year or two ago, David Reiley was elected mayor. I asked one of the old-timers what he thought about having a Catholic mayor. He replied, "Now that you mention it, I suppose he is Irish and probably Catholic. Why do you ask?"

At that election, each of the "mainline" churches had had a small notice in the Sunday bulletin: "Remember to vote on Tuesday" or something like that. None of them said anything about papism in the sermon. At the Baptist Church, however, there was a pointed reminder of where the candidates for election stood on abortion, capital punishment, and prayer in the schools.

Parallel changes were happening among the Lutherans. The young people demanded English services. Their elders wanted to continue as they always had. After much debate, some anger, and a great deal of sadness, an arrangement was worked out: English at nine and German at eleven. After a further round of agonizing, the order was switched: German at nine and English at eleven. A visitor might have noticed that the people at the German service sang lustily in German, though some had a hard time finding the hymn if the pastor occasionally forgot to announce the number in both languages. After the service, the chit-chat was all in English. A few more years, and the German service was reduced to once a month. Finally it died a natural death, and no one even noticed.

Catechism, the sole form of religious education under Pastor Weisgerber, gave way to a Sunday School hardly distinguishable from any other Sunday School, except that the materials mostly came from a Lutheran publishing house. At the same time, the "mainline" churches were abandoning the International Uniform Lessons for newer materials. Recently, Central United has started using *The Whole People of God* curriculum, supplemented by some Lutheran publications, and St. James now has a curriculum library with materials from several sources. From this the Christian Education Committee—not the pastor—makes a rather eclectic choice.

The growing Lutheran congregation built a new stone church, on the edge of town, with a large parking lot and all modern facilities. The sign

now reads "St. James Evangelical Lutheran Church." The old sign is in a storeroom; one of the members thought it might be nice to have on hand for the hundredth anniversary. The pastor before the present one was Rev. Allan McGrath. A few people wondered how anyone with a name like that got into the Lutheran ministry. But no one even raised the question when Rev. Allistair Smith was called.

Actually, his background was as soundly Lutheran as you can get. His great grandfather, Pfarrer [German for "Pastor"] Gerhardt Schmidt, was educated at University of Erlangen and came to North America to pastor a little church in a small prairie town. He was never known to use English in the church for any purpose. But his son grew up knowing both English and German, his grandson only English. During the war, this third Schmidt re-spelled the family name "Smith" and later picked a first name for his own son that would have no German flavor. Though the family gradually drifted away from German roots, they stayed strongly Lutheran. That was not as difficult as it sounds. Lutheranism, as a whole, was assimilating too—their church pretty much in step with the majority of its members.

Across the continent, the old barriers between evangelicalism, immigrant confessionalism (Lutheran and other continental-origin churches), and Roman Catholicism were breaking down. The churches began, cautiously at first, to interact. Allistair Smith, as I noted earlier, is an active participant in the ministerial association, and in the smaller group that gets together each week to study the lectionary passages for the next Sunday. Fr. Walter Steinbrenner, Fr. Mangione's successor at St. Patrick's, cooperates with the ministerial association in various projects, and even drops in on the lectionary group now and then. He is a young man, in his first parish. The seminary he attended is now federated with a Protestant seminary, and he took some of his courses from Protestant professors.

Religion in Springfield is not, however, finally coming together. New groups have been appearing as fast as old have become assimilated. A new wave of German immigration produced a small New Apostolic Church in Springfield. They stay strictly to themselves. A congregation of Jehovah's Witnesses have their little Kingdom Hall off on a back street where few see it. They too have nothing to do with the other

churches, though they are well known, as they stand on the busy street corners with their literature, or ring doorbells through the town.
There is an ever-increasing number of "unchurched." (A cynic might say that old Henry Withers had been the most successful evangelist of all!) Some of these "unchurched" are drop-outs from the old churches. Some are newcomers who have not started going to church in Springfield. Some are persons of quite different backgrounds who would affiliate, if there were a church of the tradition in which they were raised.

In the old days, most people like these would have gone to some church regularly. The neighbors, the boss, and the community busybodies expected to see them going to worship every week.

Now the boss considers that it's none of his business what his employees do on Sunday. The churches are less concerned too. The Presbyterian presiding elder, and his neighbor, the United Church Sunday School superintendent, play bridge every Sunday evening. They are in their places Sunday morning, of course. Neither church has an evening service anymore.

Some of the "unchurched" are indifferent; some are hostile. Many who consider themselves "Christians" prefer TV preaching. There are lax members, on the rolls but rarely attending. There are "adherents," very active in some church, but for one reason or another not actually members. The lines between church people and non-church people are fuzzy, and getting fuzzier.

Henry Withers was something of an oddity in his day. There are now too many of his kind to be thought of as exceptions any more. The "unchurched" are a conspicuous element in Springfield society.

W hen the "boat people" first came to the attention in North America, Central United Church and St. Patrick's Catholic Church each sponsored a family. Then St. James Lutheran Church heard that another branch of "St. Patrick's family" was in desperate need in a refugee camp. The Lutheran social action committee talked it over with their congregation and with the committee from St. Patrick's. The next thing they knew, the two congregations were working closely together on an

almost daily basis. The boat people had made their first contribution to change in Springfield.

In a town where everyone had been of European descent as long as anyone could remember, these three Vietnamese-Chinese families were something new. It took a while for everyone to adjust to it. But they did. The Phongs—they had become the "Phongs," not the "St. Patrick's family"—saved their money, and opened a little restaurant. For a while they served mostly fried chicken and chop suey. Their clientele broadened slowly, and the more adventuresome tried other dishes.

Springfield was becoming more cosmopolitan. The supermarket even began selling mangoes.

Nobody thought much of it when Dr. Ashok Rajgopal set up a practice, or when Seiji Takahashi arrived from the home office to start up and operate a new gearshift-knob factory.

A host of small changes in population have come, mostly in the last decade or two. They add up. Springfield was growing, but it was becoming more diverse. Nobody thinks of it as a "Christian town" anymore.

That is partly because "Christian" has taken on different meanings. It has acquired a very precise meaning at Lighthouse and the Baptist Church, where "Are you a Christian?" seems a perfectly natural inquiry to make of a visitor. It preserves, sharpened somewhat, the classical evangelical distinction between the evangelizers and the evangelizees.

"Are you a Christian?" might embarrass a visitor from the United or Presbyterian churches. That part of their evangelical background has been largely forgotten.

The word "Christian" has not dropped out of the vocabulary at Central United. Chalmers and his congregation alike are merely reluctant to use it to classify people. "Christian world view" or "Christian ethics" are quite in order, however, and "Christian church" is a commonplace.

No one remembers exactly when they stopped saying grace at the firemen's picnic, nor when they ceased having prayers at the grammar-school graduation. Most of these public duties of the clergy were quietly dropped.

The ministers no longer have better access to the city leaders than other respectable citizens. They are no longer called on for counsel on the urgent problems of the day. Instead, the city council hires a consultant at $200 an hour, who, a month or so later, submits a report that there are more cars coming downtown than there are parking places, and that it is worst at peak business times, and hopeless just before Christmas. The city leaders are grateful, because it confirms what they suspected all along. The report then recommends buying 25 more parking meters, and widening the street in front of the hospital.

Wesley Chalmers tried his own approach. He put an item into the Central United newsletter suggesting that the members offer their neighbor a ride to church, car pool for grocery shopping, and cut down on unnecessary trips. This, he suggested, would not only help with parking, but also reduce acid rain and save the environment. The jury is still out on which approach is most effective.

The greatest change (from our perspective, at least) has been within the churches rooted in classical evangelicalism. It started much earlier than any of the changes listed above. Actually, the first little cracks appeared while the evangelical consensus I described in the last chapter was just getting started. Even as the old divisions between Congregationalists and Methodists, Presbyterians and Baptists were beginning to be blunted, evangelicalism was starting to rift internally along new lines.

I can only mention a few highlights. The full story would be long and repetitive to the point of boredom. The same quarrel arose, over and over, first in this church then in that. Generally, they reached some sort of a truce. Then, in a slightly different shape, it would break out again.

The first major conflict was a confrontation within the Presbyterian denomination, between Princeton Seminary in New Jersey and Union Seminary in New York. All Presbyterians involved in denominational structures were forced to take sides, and many others did so voluntarily. Princeton came to be known as "conservative" and Union as "liberal." This was a great advantage for the Princeton-led faction, because the question was, in the simplest terms, which theologians were faithful to the teachings of Calvin and the Westminster Confession on the nature and authority of Scripture. Presbyterians were innately inclined to revere, protect, and follow those teachings. So almost from the beginning the Princeton theologians had the upper hand as "conservatives."

Princeton won the first round, when Professor Charles A. Briggs of Union was dismissed from the Presbyterian ministry, basically for his support of the new biblical scholarship coming out of Germany. The seminary refused to dismiss him, and the church severed its relationship with Union. That was in 1893. At the same session, the Presbyterian Church's General Assembly further ruled:

> The Bible as we now have it, in its various translations and versions, when freed from all errors and mistakes of translators, copyists, and printers, is the very Word of God and consequently wholly without error.

That was a much stronger official statement than had ever been made before. It introduced a new phrase, "wholly without error," notably absent from the Westminster confession.

All that was an internal matter within the Presbyterian Church in the United States of America. As it developed, however, the conflict was followed closely in other Presbyterian branches and in other denominations in both Canada and the U.S., especially those, like the Congregational and Baptist, that had a Calvinist background.

The "conservative" triumph in 1893 did not settle the matter, even within that Presbyterian denomination. Knox Springfield's representatives at presbytery sat through debates, sometimes understanding what was at stake, sometimes not, often deeply torn. They brought some of their anxieties back to the congregation. On the whole, Knox Church in Springfield was loyal to their denomination above anything else, and went along, however things worked out.

Surprisingly, after gaining ground for several decades, the "conservatives" suddenly lost control of the Presbyterian Church in the U.S.A. in the '20s. That, too, was felt across the sister Presbyterian churches and some other denominations. Again, Knox, out of denominational loyalty, went along. When the lines were finally drawn in Springfield, Knox found itself on the "liberal" side, though only a few of the members really understood why.

Over roughly the same period, North America was racked by a second controversy—evolution. Darwin's theory was seen as conflicting with a common interpretation of the Bible. This new controversy got entangled with the other. The passions engendered were pooled.

It is hard to think of a controversy better suited to caricature and misrepresentation. Evolution was commonly understood to teach that man was descended from monkeys. The comment of one Springfield church member was about as informed as any: "For my side of the family, I deny it; for Bob's side, I am not so sure."

Every church in Springfield was divided, though the balance differed. Only a minority of the Congregationalists were confirmed opponents of evolution, but a majority of the Baptists were. The rest were mostly noncommittal, until the Scopes Trial in 1925 and all the attendant discussion pretty well forced people to take sides.

The battle was not *between* the churches, but *within* each. Each church made efforts to hold its congregation together, but sooner or later breaks came. Not one of the churches in Springfield actually split, though that did happen in some nearby towns. Rather, one family would shift allegiance, and the next year another. When there was a minor dispute about some totally unrelated matter—for example, in the Methodist church one year over new carpeting in the sanctuary—two or three families would take it as a good excuse to transfer.

The upshot was that the staunch anti-evolutionists among the Congregationalists gradually transferred their membership, mostly to the Baptists, and the pro-evolutionists among the Baptists ended up scattered among the other three churches.

In the process, the Baptists became ever more firmly committed to "the biblical account of Creation" and "the inerrancy of the Bible."

The Scopes Trial was the grand finale of the controversy. By the time it came along, the three other evangelical churches in Springfield had pretty well settled where they stood: churches should stay out of scientific controversies. The Baptists in Springfield were equally certain that they must dig in and defend "the biblical account" to the last ditch. In some other communities Baptist churches went the other way, and in some they divided. The denomination was split.

In the fall of 1910, Deacon Abner Johnson of the Baptist church bought a new Bible from a traveling Bible salesman. It was something different from anything he had seen before: the same old Bible, but with a marvelous set of notes and other aids. He found that it gave him a great deal of help in preparing for the adult Sunday School lesson he taught every week; it was a great supplement to the quarterlies. It cleared up a lot of questions that had bothered him for years. It made everything fit together. It opened up new truths about the times "soon to come."

Deacon Johnson had bought *The Scofield Reference Bible*, edited by C. I. Scofield and published just the year before. It claimed to have been compiled on the basis of "thirty years' study and use of the Scriptures as pastor, teacher, writer, and lecturer upon biblical themes." It seemed to Deacon Johnson that Scofield had been doing just exactly his kind of Bible study—or rather just the kind that he had always wanted to do. Scofield had been extremely successful in working out the knotty problems, and making them clear for people like the members of Calvary Baptist Church—people who "stood fast on the Bible."

The same characteristics that endeared *Scofield* to Deacon Johnson made most of the other churches first dubious and then antagonistic. It seemed too glib, too dogmatic, and in a few places simply ridiculous. The few copies that found their way into Congregational hands—those Bible salesmen could be mighty convincing—either helped carry their owners over to the Baptists, or soon sat unused on the shelf.

On Deacon Johnson's recommendation, many more Baptists bought *The Scofield Reference Bible*. They began to rely more and more on its notes. That soon clinched the matter. It gave them a basis to organize their Bible knowledge.

That basis was dispensationalism. Dispensationalism was, in part, a way of interpreting the Bible. It was also a special vision of the end-times as presented in Daniel and Revelation, a specific variety of premillenialism.

Dispensationalists put heavy emphasis on prophecy, reading as prophetic many Bible passages that others would not. They draw a careful distinction between Israel and the Church, some prophecies applying to one and some to the other. "Rightly dividing the word of truth" (2 Timothy 2:15) was taken as a watchword. Christ will return to "rapture" the saints. There will be a period of tribulation. Then the millenium will fulfill the promises made to Abraham and Israel. "Premillenialism" labels the belief in this general order of events. All dispensationalists are premillenial; not all premillenialists are dispensational.

The full scheme is, of course, intricate. Many adherents seem to revel in the intricacies, all, they claim, established by minute study of the Bible.

Dispensationalism was everywhere linked closely with inerrancy. And increasingly, inerrancy became linked to dispensationalism. The combination formed one of the central varieties of what was emerging as the fundamentalist movement. Calvary Baptist found new anchorage within that movement. Its sign now reads:

CALVARY BAPTIST CHURCH
A Bible Believing Church
Sunday School 9:30
Worship 11:00
and 7:00
Prayer Meeting, Wednesday 7:00
INDEPENDENT, FUNDAMENTAL, PREMILLENIAL

Just as in Calvary Baptist Church, all across North America dispensationalism gave a coherence to the anti-critical, anti-evolution wing of the old evangelicalism. The core of the movement took it up and built on it. The *Scofield Reference Bible* had a key part in this. Many supporting books, magazines, movements, and institutions grew up. Important among them were the Bible schools such as The Word. Generally they taught dispensationalism.

Dispensational fundamentalism is by no means the only theological position on that side of the great division, but it has been the dominant one. Most adherents have shifted somewhat from many of the interpretations in the *Scofield Reference Bible*. But Scofield's general framework stands as an integrating force within fundamentalism.

Inerrancy supported by dispensationalism seems to its supporters to make the faith firm and immovable, a landmark in troubled times.

In the inheritance which you will hold in the land that the Lord your God gives you to possess, you shall not remove your neighbor's landmark, which the men of old have set. (Deuteronomy 19:14, RSV)

The "mainline" churches—or better the "mainline" within the major churches—had nothing like *Scofield* to mark out a stand for them, nothing like dispensationalism around which a coherent movement could be built.

By the nature of the case, they could not. The path they chose was that of remaining more or less open to new developments in society, in science, and in scholarly study of the Bible. That, of course, gave them no fixed point. The world is moving faster than ever before. Science has exploded. Scholarship continually shifts—some scholars like to think that all the shifting is progress.

The old classical evangelicalism took, without much debate, the

Bible to be authoritative in matters religious, moral, *and* civil. No church, and very few individuals, rejected that authority outright. Many, however, began to rethink the questions, generally concentrating on one end of the formula: What is religious and what not?

Meanwhile the "civil" end was *tacitly* redefined. Dropping the grace at the firemen's picnic was only a small thing, but it symbolized a change that has been going on relentlessly. The church and the Bible are excluded more and more from North American public life. The movement is selective, but decisive. The civil authority of the Bible is being redefined, not by the churches but by society at large.

In this fluid situation, some have come to see that the Bible itself rather than any doctrine about the Bible is the only guide. It could be no unmoving, immutable Bible, but the living Word, moving before them into new situations, constantly heard anew.

And the Lord went before them by day in a pillar of cloud to lead them along the way, and by night in a pillar of fire to give them light, that they might travel by day and by night. (Exodus 13:21, RSV)

THE EVANGELICAL HERITAGE

All across the church the Sunday School is declining. A few suggest that it is about time we find an alternative. Most merely lament the decline. Others speculate about the causes. The birth rate is falling. Hockey teams have discovered Sunday morning as possible practice time. Children are less easily herded into activities their parents choose.

It is a recent decline. Three or four decades ago, the Sunday Schools were booming. Let's go back and look at the Sunday School then. We have had brief introductions to two examples: Trinity Sunday School, where Wesley Chalmers went, and Love One Another Sunday School, where G. Whitefield Finney got his start.

Reginald Scott was the superintendent at Trinity Sunday School in Barnesborough. Of course, he was also a member of Trinity United Church, but for him that was more or less incidental. Apart from his family and his small hardware store, Trinity Sunday School was his whole life. The church was an appendage to the Sunday School, necessary, of course, but quite secondary.

Mr. Scott never went to church; he was busy every Sunday morning in his Sunday School. Indeed, he was there at least half an hour before anyone else and always the last to leave the building. He was a conscientious superintendent, insisting that every detail be in order when the teachers and children arrived, and all the equipment put away and the records completed before he left.

Mrs. Scott used to report to him about the morning sermon. He listened carefully. He was sometimes irked because the minister spent so much time on that theology stuff. Social issues irritated him even more. He wished the pastor would stick closer to the Bible. They didn't have an adult class anymore, and where else would they get it if the sermon didn't give it to them?

Mrs. Scott was also a loyal member of the Church Women. She would report, too, about their activities. Reginald listened patiently, but with less real interest. It was not that he didn't appreciate women and their work. Indeed, he valued their help. They washed, dressed, fed, and

delivered his children to him every Sunday morning. They kept those children in good health and feeling loved until next Sunday. The best of them helped his charges with their memory verses, and showed proper appreciation for the handwork they brought home. Reginald Scott had a good knowledge of the Bible. There was scarcely a story in it which he could not tell in full detail. But he did not rest on his accomplishments. He read the Bible, and he studied the quarterlies. In fact he subscribed on his own to two others. They gave him some helpful hints not in the quarterly series he bought for the teachers.

He puzzled over the application of each story to his children. It isn't always easy to find the moral. But there must be one, he believed.

He prepared carefully for each Sunday, and especially for the teachers' meetings every Tuesday. He saw it as giving them the help they needed and the inspiration to teach with enthusiasm. Most of the teachers realized it was really more than that. His teaching had to be their substitute for the morning sermon. The teachers appreciated the insights he gave them. They sometimes felt that they were the most fortunate ones in the congregation.

Imogene Finney didn't have quite as much time for preparation as Reginald Scott. It took a lot of work keeping a home going on the meager income Amos made. But she and her husband regularly read the Bible together every day. They prayed about it and they talked about it. She listened attentively to her husband's preaching, and they talked about that afterwards too. It was part of her life to support him in his ministry, and he was glad for her support and occasional suggestions.

The only thing she did on her own was to read the quarterlies conscientiously in advance of each Sunday, and then think about their suggestions as she went about her washing and cooking and cleaning.

She never spoke of "my Sunday School" anything like the way Reginald Scott did. It was part of "our church," the part given to her stewardship.

Reginald Scott knew the superintendents of most of the other churches in Barnesborough. Whenever one of them came into his hardware store, he would take a few minutes to compare notes, exchange ideas, and just hear how things were going. He always tried to find a slack time to go to the post office. That way he could chat a minute or two with the postmaster about his Sunday School at the Nazarene Church.

Things were different when Scott first took over Trinity's Sunday School. In those days they had a Sunday School teachers' rally for Barnes County every year. A couple of hundred leaders from all kinds of churches would gather for a Saturday. They would have a Bible study, morning and afternoon. There would be a session on some aspect of Sunday School work. For each, they could generally get an editor from some quarterly series, or the superintendent of some outstanding Sunday School, or a well-known adult-class teacher, or some other challenging lay speaker. Only rarely did they have to settle for a preacher. There would be reports from all parts of the county. And dinner together. It was a great help and inspiration.

Reginald Scott thought it was great that they could get together from "all" the churches. He never noticed that the participants in all these affairs were strictly from the right side of the tracks.

Over in Middlefield they had similar events. But Imogene Finney never went; in fact she usually didn't even hear about them.

Not so long ago, in some churches the adult class outdrew the morning worship. Adult Sunday School teachers might acquire a reputation far beyond their own school. They would be in demand to speak at Sunday School rallies and other special events. Occasionally two of them would exchange for a Sunday. The class members enjoyed the opportunity of hearing another eloquent teacher.

These famous teachers, of course, usually had no training as such. They had the same self-taught knowledge of the Bible as Reginald Scott. Like him, they also had drawn on the pool of experience of other teachers. Many of them were lawyers or judges, broadly educated people with training in public speaking. Their real skill was in presentation.

The adult class lasted longest in the U.S. South. In the 1950s some adult classes drew a thousand or more every Sunday and were broadcast to many thousands more. One governor was generally considered to have won election on the basis of the state-wide following he had built up over many years as a radio Sunday School teacher.

Sunday School, as Reginald Scott knew it, was a direct inheritance from classical evangelicalism. In old Springfield the Sunday Schools were run in much the same way. There was a county Sunday School Union, and it brought all the major Sunday Schools together. The superintendents and some of the teachers—of the adult classes particularly—had their informal network.

Histories credit the first Sunday School to Robert Raikes in England in 1781. He would not have recognized Springfield's Sunday Schools. They had been drastically re-formed by North American evangelicalism. At the same time, they had contributed at least as much as any other institution to creating that evangelical consensus. That they led was evident: the four evangelical Sunday Schools in Springfield were almost identical at a time when the church services still preserved some ancient denominational peculiarities. The Sunday Schools were, in fact, one of the chief forces pulling the evangelical community together.

Many small communities did not have enough people of any one denomination to organize a church, but there were enough children to have a Sunday School. Thousands of community Sunday Schools flourished across the continent. They were entirely non-denominational. One teacher might be a Baptist, another a Methodist, and another a Presbyterian. But they wore no identifying badges. Sunday morning most of them traveled to their church outside the community. Sunday afternoon they met together and taught side by side. Such a Sunday School might meet in the school house, or in someone's home. Some built little chapels strictly for Sunday School use.

These community Sunday Schools were clear indications of the non-sectarian trend in classical evangelicalism. The churches and the clergy had no part in them. They reveled in their independence, and easily became anti-denominational.

Community Sunday Schools—and Sunday School cooperation in general—were possible, first, because the churches all used a common Bible. One of the most important accomplishments of an earlier age had been the near unanimous adoption of the King James Version. Few people in old Springfield had any idea that the Bible had ever been other than their familiar King James.

The common Bible made possible that inscription over the door to Springfield High School, "Ye shall know the truth, and the truth shall

YE SHALL KNOW THE TRUTH
AND THE TRUTH SHALL MAKE YOU FREE

make you free." It was a major part of the platform from which developed all that civil involvement of the churches and clergy in old Springfield.

Second, cooperation was possible because a distinction was tacitly established between the Bible text and its interpretation. On text, all could agree. On interpretation, they *expected* differences, and they were prepared to *accept* differences. For extremists, the differences were not important because they were denomination-based; denominations are not biblical.

The Sunday Schools stressed the text, particularly the non-controversial parts. So did the schools, the general public, and the civil authorities. If any verse of denominational significance came up, the Sunday Schools generally skirted the issue.

Bible Societies had been working in North America for a couple of generations and had contributed greatly to that understanding. They had been founded to encourage and assist the distribution of the Bible "without note or comment." In a continent where denominations were at war, the Bible Societies strove to be strictly neutral. They considered that the Bible could stand on its own, with no need of dogmatic underpinning. Somehow that appealed; they had the support of lay people in most of the major churches.

Cooperative Sunday School work made its greatest mark through the development of the International Uniform Lessons, started in 1872. These listed for each Sunday a passage to be studied in all the churches. The Sunday Schools put heavy emphasis on consistent attendance with annual awards. Those persons who had to travel could now go to Sunday School wherever they were and maintain the continuity, and they could

take back an attendance certificate to keep their attendance records intact.

The selected passages of the Uniform Lessons were organized into quarters, each following some theme through the thirteen Sundays: the life of David, Paul's journey to Rome, the Sermon on the Mount... The committee picked the passages. Various publishers produced the actual materials, universally known as "quarterlies."

Some of the publishers were denominational; they were free to give a peculiarly denominational interpretation. Others were non-denominational, but they too would impose whatever interpretation was in line with their policy. There is a parallel here to the Bible Societies' "without note or comment." Text and interpretation were separated.

The plan called for one lesson each quarter on temperance. So, if the quarter covered the life of David, for example, some instance in his life would be selected that allowed a temperance lesson to be drawn. In some quarters, it took some ingenuity to find a way. They always did.

Those temperance lessons were indicative. The scheme was skewed toward superficial moralizing. It often forced passages to address an issue foreign to their original intent. Teachers often accentuated that skewing.

It was also skewed toward stories. Of course other materials were included, but most of the teachers found the stories easier to teach, and most of the members found them easier to understand. Passages with direct practical application were preferred over the more abstract.

The system had little place for any broad outlines. Abraham, David, and Paul were commonly presented against the same background, minimally different from contemporary North America.

The result was a distinctive approach to the Bible. Often it differed from the approach in the sermons in small but significant ways. A division between church and Sunday School took root very early in classical evangelicalism, and deepened over the years. It blossomed in the disjointedness that so characterizes life in the United churches. This is part of *their* evangelical inheritance.

Fundamentalist churches stand in that same heritage. Why do they not also show this disjointedness? I don't know, but I have a guess.

Much of their inheritance reaches them through small, spontaneous churches like Love One Another Tabernacle. It is not typical that the preacher and the Sunday School superintendent are husband and wife. But it is usual that the preachers and lay leadership stand close together, much closer than in the larger churches. Both work within the same vision for the church.

In a way, the Sunday morning at the Tabernacle was one long service with a brief intermission in the middle. The two were completely compatible, and well integrated. There was no segregation of story in the Sunday School and theology in the church service. If a verse came along that was best interpreted doctrinally, the teachers went bravely on. The Sunday School put it all in the framework of the saving Blood, the soon Return, and the inerrant Word, just as the preaching did.

At Trinity, and most United Church Sunday Schools, lay teachers felt inadequate to handle most theological questions, and tended to avoid them. They felt more at home with the stories.

L ast time I heard anything about Reginald Scott, he was much concerned. A United Church in a nearby town was setting up a ministerial team consisting of a pastor and a minister of Christian education. He saw the teaming as an attempt by the clergy to take over the Sunday School. He felt very strongly that the Sunday School should be autonomous.

Needless to say, that church board didn't see it quite the same way. They felt that the Sunday School needed pepping up and modernizing. They counted on new leadership to make it more relevant and more interesting. Especially, they wanted it to be better integrated into the total program of the church.

That was exactly what scared Scott. He saw integration as less Bible, more of that other stuff that kept coming into the sermons. To be biblical was to stick with the text and its obvious moral, not to wander off into theological interpretation.

Members of the Trinity congregation had heard about that new appointment. Some of them wondered whether Trinity could get a Christian Education director too. Talking among themselves, they suggested that Reginald Scott was too conservative for their tastes. One of them even raised the question whether he might be a "fundamentalist." Of course, he was not. If by "conservative" they meant theologically conservative, he really wasn't that either. Bible knowledge he had in abundance, but not enough theological knowledge to allow classification. He stood for inherited ways of doing things, not for anything deeper.

Reginald Scott was, however, open to recruitment by any movement that came along, "liberal," "conservative," or whatever. It only needed to argue from the Bible the way he knew it. A passage out of context would be fine; he was, in fact, a little distrustful of wider settings. Moralizing would be fine; looking at it in a broader theological framework made him uncomfortable.

Trinity United Church did not get a Christian Education Director. But soon after that crisis, Reginald Scott retired from the superintendency. The minister then at Trinity, with consummate diplomacy, got a Christian Development Committee appointed, and saw to it that the committee represented the whole church—there were two high school students on it. They started a Tuesday night Bible study, and revitalized the young people's association.

Then they made a few minor suggestions to the Sunday School. The pastor guided them in working very discreetly; she knew the dangers of any appearance of meddling. Gradually the committee caught some of the pastor's vision and accepted many of her ideas. Their influence expanded.

It worked. In a few years, all of Scott's old teachers had either retired or been won over. One of the older teachers moved in the church's annual meeting that the committee be renamed "Christian Education and Development Committee" and be asked to guide the Sunday School. The school soon had a new curriculum. Most important, it was now operating as a part of the whole congregation. It had become quite open to further change as needed.

Old Springfield had four non-sectarian Christian institutions.

One was the Sunday School movement, which had branches in each of the churches. (The churches didn't think of them that way, of course!) But its superstructure was non-denominational: county unions, regional unions, and over it all the American Sunday School Union.

The second was the Bible Society. Though independent of the churches, it appealed each year to each congregation for funds, and it was supported by most. It also had an auxiliary in Springfield. The annual meeting was always interesting and inspirational. It involved some very influential people. With the backing of the Society, they worked for more Bible reading whenever the opportunity came up. It was the Bible itself they pushed, not interpretation.

The third group, the Young Men's Christian Association and the Young Women's Christian Association, was even less tied to the churches. Their funds came directly from their members and friends. Their efforts were directed to reaching young people with the Gospel. Several leaders in Springfield gave the YMCA or the YWCA credit for leading them to Christ. Their version of the Gospel was as thoroughly stripped of denominational trappings as they could make it.

The Springfield town council perpetually agonized over the "drinking problem" and got nowhere. The Women's Christian Temperance Union, the fourth of these non-sectarian institutions, took action They worked with and for the family victims of drunkenness. They campaigned against the taverns, and against the bootleggers that everyone except the constable seemed to know about. They reminded candidates for public office that the evangelical public wanted results. The WCTU was at this time the only expression in Springfield of the evangelical drive for social justice which had earlier pushed the churches and general public opinion in Springfield toward abolition. It was an organization of church people, but was completely independent of the churches. Unlike the YMCA/YWCA, the WCTU was looked on with suspicion by some of the church pillars.

Many more such movements had not reached Springfield. Almost without exception they were:
a) Bible based
b) Lay led
c) Non-sectarian
d) Sharply focused on some particular work
e) Evangelistic in intent
f) In the vanguard of evangelical consensus and unity.

These societies were almost the sole means for individual members of different churches to work together. They were the only vehicle of interchurch cooperation, and so the major instrument in pulling the churches into the consensus we call "evangelicalism."

At a later time, they became known as "parachurch" organizations or "parachurch" movements.

Classical evangelicalism was based on two commitments: to the Bible and to evangelization. It saw the population divided into saved and unsaved. Its ultimate task was moving people from the unsaved category into the saved. That task fell to the saved as a whole—they didn't necessarily think of them as the "church." Evangelization was not to be left to the clergy, or even to the churches. In the thinking of most of the parachurch organizations, it was a lay responsibility. The Sunday School, for example, was not merely a teaching institution; its commission was to lead people to Christ. Few thought of it as the task of the church and Sunday School working together. Its evangelistic commitment would affect the way it taught. The immediate task of teaching Bible would affect the Sunday School's understanding of evangelism, and so of conversion, and of the Christian life.

Every traveler knows the Gideon Bible. A few years ago, you could find one in every hotel room. Since roughly the turn of the century, placing Bibles has been the major undertaking of the Gideons, one of those parachurch organizations. The motivation is evangelistic, the strategy almost mechanical—to lead people to Christ, you must lead them to the Bible. A lonely traveler in a hotel room will read whatever is at hand. With just a little guidance—there are suggested passages to read—Bible reading will start the process; indeed, it may lead to conversion.

Dedication to the task of providing Bibles has pushed the Gideons toward assuming that reading the Bible will, by itself, produce conversion. The Bible becomes a tool, evangelization moves away from the church, and conversion becomes an impersonal process. These shifts ran through many of the parachurch movements.

Nineteenth century evangelicalism also domesticated evangelization within the churches. It tamed the old fire and brimstone preaching of the frontier. It gave "preaching for a decision" a decorous place in the order of things. It put great emphasis on means—Bibles, tracts, the new gospel songs...

It tamed conversion into an expected routine, the standard way one entered the church. It regularized the mechanism: evangelistic services Sunday evenings, "revival meeting" every summer. The patterns varied from area to area, but everywhere there was a movement toward routine. Only the occasional infusion of new vigor from other sources saved evangelism from complete conventionalization.

Evangelicalism ultimately broke apart. When the will was probated, this commitment to evangelization with decency and order was distributed among the heirs. The parachurch organizations which fostered it had various destinies. The local Sunday Schools were so tied to the churches that they went into every faction. The overall structure tried to maintain neutrality. The International Uniform Lessons continued in use in both fundamental and "liberal" churches. In the latter, they ultimately contributed to the kind of disjointedness described earlier.

The YMCA and YWCA gradually lost their evangelistic mission and then their Christian orientation. Today few know what the C stands for, and those who do wonder how it ever got there. Still, they have maintained the respect of the churches.

The WCTU became the nucleus of an expanding political coalition that made itself felt in politics and in community attitudes. It continued to think of its work as an expression of Christian morality and social imperative. It was, however, never close to the churches, and continued to be opposed by some of them. It opened the way for later advocacy groups dealing with peace and justice.

The Bible Societies maintained both their neutrality and their wide support. Both Central United Church and Lighthouse Bible Church contribute each year. Some members of each attend the district meetings, now held in a nearby larger town. It is the only direct contact members of the two churches have in a Christian context.

Most of the other surviving parachurch organizations went definitely with the fundamentalists or with similar factions. They have proliferated at an accelerating rate, and new types have appeared.

The parachurch pattern has become characteristic of this side. It is the evangelical way of expressing unity. It does so, in part, by disregarding or downplaying denominations.

The mainline body also inherited a desire for unity, but had to work out new forms to express it. The United Church of Canada and the United Church of Christ are prime examples of one form. The National Council of Churches of Christ in the United States of America and the Canadian Council of Churches are another. Both are agencies for cooperation between denominations.

The heirs of the old evangelicalism have different ways of organizing themselves, different cultures. But both are rooted in their common heritage.

MODERN EVANGELICALISM

Evangelicalism broke apart on the twin issues of evolution and biblical criticism. One vocal party took up the name "fundamental," which they generally interpreted to mean that they stood solidly and uncompromisingly for the "fundamental truths of Christianity": the verbal inspiration of Scripture, the divinity of Christ, the virgin birth, the physical resurrection, and the substitutionary atonement—or some such list.

In Springfield the break-up left two factions. Calvary Baptist Church went with the fundamentalists, the other churches with the "mainline." In the wider world there were many more fragments. No one realized quite how many, because at each crisis a pair of coalitions would form, one pro and one con. This gave the appearance that there was just one line of division. Any factions that succeeded in standing aside were hardly noticed.

"Fundamentalist" became one of those symbolic labels. Treasured and honored within, it was used outside, often inaccurately, as a term of abuse. United Church people who are concerned about fairness in language should try to eliminate the pejorative uses of this label, but not the label itself—for it is not theirs to dispose of.

The fundamentalists dubbed their opponents "modernists," "liberals" (a term that has never had good press in the U.S.), "social gospelites," and so forth. None of these terms really stuck, except among the fundamentalists, who did not use them as compliments.

This major non-fundamentalist mass never felt self-conscious enough to create its own label. No label appeared that even a sizable minority could embrace. I have called it "mainline"; the only good thing about the term is that it is, presumably, innocuous.

With the break-up of the evangelical consensus came the inevitable scrap over the assets. Factions fought for control of denominational structures, of colleges and seminaries, of parachurch organizations, of publishing houses, and of local churches. One of the most valuable assets went almost unnoticed, the name "evangelical."

In the '40s a newly emerging coalition of fragments remembered the name "evangelical" and staked a claim to it. The name became theirs, and with it the appearance of being the sole heir of classical evangelicalism.

This modern evangelicalism became a growing force in North American Protestantism. It somehow got good press, and came to be widely heralded as the most vital, most rapidly growing, and generally most successful wing of the church. It continues to get a great deal of media attention.

These evangelicals put much effort into building a sense of identity and a positive self-image. They exploited new technologies in exciting ways. They made good use of their name and its claim to great roots. They had something to offer to Christians who had felt left behind or caught in a church that was going nowhere.

This modern evangelical movement originally brought together two groups: Some were ex-fundamentalists, people who had become disenchanted with the narrowness of the fundamentalism they knew, but still held a strongly Bible-centered faith. Some had never been fundamentalists but held what seemed to them a more strongly biblical faith than prevailed in the mainline denominations. They came together on common ground in the Bible. They set out to bring together all who showed similar biblical allegiance.

Lighthouse boasts, "We preach the Bible uncompromised," and Calvary Baptist proclaims on its sign that it is "A Bible-believing church." Many such churches slowly relaxed their strict separatism. They became more open to others who differed only slightly, while still maintaining their strong opposition to "modernists."

The evangelical coalition sought, generally successfully, to bring in such Bible-promoting churches. Much of the fundamentalist movement found a place within the larger evangelical framework. Once in, their outlook has slowly broadened. Only the most narrowly separatist fundamentalists stayed out.

Growth continued as new factions joined. There were, for example, the Pentecostals. These churches originated about the turn of the century as a revival movement coming out of the older churches. For some decades they looked on the older churches, fundamental, liberal or whatever, as lifeless. In turn, they were rejected by the fundamentalists as unsound in doctrine, and they were disparaged by the mainline churches as disorderly.

Pentecostals were and are strongly biblical, with a special emphasis on the leading of the Holy Spirit as they read the Scriptures. By the time the evangelical coalition gathered strength, the differences could be overlooked. A large segment of the Pentecostal movement was welcomed into evangelicalism.

The mainline denominations all had a spectrum ranging from "liberal" to "conservative." Those at the "conservative" end often felt themselves discriminated against or neglected. The new evangelical movement provided for them, too, both an identity and a link to others. Many accepted a double affiliation: organizationally they were in a denomination, informally they were evangelicals.

Evangelicalism today includes denominations, local churches of mainline denominations, non-denominational churches, a wide range of institutions and businesses, and individuals. Their denominational roots are various, and their theological stands are diverse in many areas. This breadth is possible because evangelicalism is largely a single issue coalition, held together by the favorable associations of their name and common beliefs about the Bible. These shared beliefs are important enough that they can override quite a range of differences.

Very few generalizations of all evangelicals or of all mainliners will hold. Yet some traits are widespread and worth noting. When any such are mentioned, it must always be understood that they are, at best, statements about *many* evangelicals, never *all*.

Bible centeredness reflects two things: their own beliefs about the Bible, and their reaction to the rejection of the Bible that they perceive in others. Like their ancestors' judgement of the Catholics and Lutherans, their appraisal of others may be superficial. But to themselves it seems well-grounded.

Such Bible loyalty has both an inclusive and an exclusive side. It brought together groups previously at odds, and it built a fence around the new grouping. Non-evangelicals need to understand both the boundary around the movement and the unity within—and the diversity behind the unity.

About the same time as the evangelical coalition was gaining strength, the terms "inerrant" and "inerrancy" became popular. Classical evangelicalism had most often used "infallible." Many of the broken fragments continued that use although, the modern evangelicals thought, they had abandoned the authority of the Bible. That rendered the word "infallible" suspect. "Inerrant" was picked up as stronger, and became the rallying cry. "Evangelicals" hold to "inerrancy" and those who hold "inerrancy" are generally expected to be "evangelicals."

"Inerrancy," however, is not the naive sort of reading that "liberals" often portray it as. The complexities are many and significant.

Fundamentalists are commonly thought of as being literalists. That is far from the case. Consider the following passage:

> The Lord God said to the serpent...I will put enmity between you and the woman, and between your seed and her seed; he shall bruise your head and you shall bruise his heel. (Genesis 3:14–15 RSV)

One evangelical interpretation is that the woman's seed is Christ, the serpent and his seed is Satan, the bruising of the serpent's head is Christ's triumph over Satan in the atonement, and the bruising of the heel is Christ's suffering on the cross.

This is far from literal. It is an example of a special technique of interpretation known as "typology." Though not every evangelical would use it here, most use it in some passages.

The distinctiveness of evangelical biblicism is more a matter of *where* interpretation is literal and where not. As a very broad generalization, evangelicals tend to be more literal when dealing with prophecy and less with other material. "Liberals" tend to treat most prophecy as poetic and/or figurative, but will interpret literally many other passages that evangelicals will treat in non-literal ways.

Another very broad generalization: Evangelicals tend to take much more of the Bible as prophecy; mainline readers take a much smaller portion to be prophetic. This is in line with the much greater interest of evangelicals, and particularly fundamentalists, in events to come.

Both generalizations must be stated in terms of tendencies, not absolutes.

While much of evangelical thinking is shaped by "inerrancy," other related ideas play important parts also. Evangelicals differ from the mainline, for example, in their stress on doctrine, in the way they see the centrality of the Gospel, and in their strong emphasis on its unchangeableness.

G. Whitefield Finney was ordained to the "Gospel ministry." That, he believes, is as it should be. A great variety of duties fall to him. He thinks of them all as somehow or other related to Gospel, to the good news of salvation in Christ Jesus. His central task is proclaiming the Gospel. Teaching true biblical doctrine is perhaps not quite the same thing, but, for him, the distinction is small.

He doesn't speak of himself as an "evangelical minister," though he is quite happy with others referring to him by the term. For him it implies that he is, in broad terms, doctrinally sound. No one can preach the Gospel effectively who is not doctrinally sound. Churches can not take their proper share in the work of proclaiming the Gospel unless they too are doctrinally sound.

Wesley Chalmers was ordained to "the ministry of Word, sacrament, and pastoral care." That seems to him to be as good a job description as anyone could state in a mere eight words. It suggests three major areas of ministry. They are, in his opinion, the central functions on which all the others depend.

The three are not wholly separate, but they are distinct. He certainly places more emphasis on "sacrament" than Finney would. Both consider "pastoral care" important; but Chalmers sees it a little more in terms of helping people, and Finney more in terms of rendering Gospel service.

Some of Chalmers' United Church colleagues would explain "ministry of Word" as the act of preaching. Chalmers prefers to think of it as communicating the Good News. That is why he generally writes "Word" with a capital. It is not his own word, but the Word, coming from outside himself. His task as a preacher is not to speak from his own wisdom, but to declare the Gospel that has been given to him and to the church. Always he must first listen. Finney wouldn't say it that way, but in general he would concur.

A third possible interpretation that would link "the ministry of Word" with teaching of doctrine does not even occur to Chalmers or most of his friends in the ministry.

Those two United Church interpretations of "the ministry of Word" are related, of course. It may even seem like a quibble to distinguish them. Yet one puts the emphasis on the form, and the other on the message. For Chalmers the distinction matters; it is the message that counts. That is why, when he starts his sermon preparation, his first step is always to read the Bible texts and then ask that question: "What is the good news in these passages for this people in this place on this day?"

Four words or phrases are closely linked in any such discussion: "Word," "good news," "Gospel," and "Evangel." They are not precise synonyms, but they come close. Grammatically, "Evangel" is unique among the four; from it a whole family of other words can be formed: "evangelical," "evangelicalism," "evangelism," "evangelist," "evangelistic," "evangelize"... That gives it a special usefulness.

Chalmers is ambivalent about this family of words. He ought to be able to speak of "evangelical, sacramental, and pastoral ministry." He would like to claim to be an "evangelical minister." Part of his work should be "evangelism." Unfortunately, all these words have acquired—or been given—special meanings that make their use embarrassing, difficult, or, occasionally, nearly impossible. "Evangelism" is often understood as labeling one specific way of proclaiming the good news—a way that Chalmers considers simplistic. "Evangelistic" is even more strongly focused on this way. Both these words are in common use around Lighthouse.

What most irks Chalmers is that "evangelical" has been appropriated as a label for a movement with which he does not feel comfortable. That makes him hesitant to use it at all.

Evangelicals are always eager to recruit, but they can't quite see Chalmers as one with themselves. If they knew more of his way of sermon preparation they might have further qualms.

It's that question he asks of himself. The first part is fine, "What is the good news in these passages...?" But "...for this people, in this place, on this day?" seems to suggest that the Gospel is relative, molded to the cultural and situational context. Any hint in this direction makes most evangelicals uneasy, to say the least.

Chalmers will freely admit that his thinking about preaching has a kind of relativism in it. He got a bit of that at Pilgrim Seminary. His first parish—in that mining town, with its special fears and tensions—strengthened it. Since then he has preached in two other communities. He has sensed differences that seemed to touch the people deeply. He has been convinced that the only way to maintain integrity in his preaching must be to adjust the message to the situation, specifically to the human plight in the situation. It is not something that he formulates into a doctrinal statement, just a gut feeling, but a powerful one.

Evangelicals, for the most part, take the Gospel to be unchanged and unchanging, eternal truth. The truth is there in the Bible, to be read out from the text, and to be preached. The mode of presentation can vary, and evangelicals do vary it. But the message is the same in a Newfoundland outport, a declining rust-belt industrial town in Pennsylvania, or a booming upper-middle-class suburb near Toronto. The graduates of Finney's Bible School all went out to churches that were much the same. Each church insulated itself from the secular culture around, in strict conformity—they thought—to Paul's injunction, "be not conformed to this world" (Romans 12:2). The world might vary, but the Gospel does not, and they must not.

United Churches do not necessarily conform to their surrounding communities, but they are not as sharply cut off. They see the task as preaching the Gospel *in* their own special situation, and *to* that situation. The one Gospel takes a different shape on the frayed edges of downtown where the residents sleep on grates, and in yuppietown where parents want their progeny baptized in Perrier. The one God of Israel gave the prophets words of hope for one audience and doom for another. The modern preacher's mandate is the same.

E vangelicals might accuse Chalmers of "conformity" and "worldliness" in his preaching. He could reply that he always asks, "What is the good news *in this passage*..." He listens for what the Bible says. He does not set the agenda, nor does he ordinarily pick the passage. He accepts the lectionary as a discipline on his *listening* and his preaching.

On occasions, he feels he has to break away from the lectionary. His people insist on a sermon for Mother's Day that fits the occasion. Then he must go to "topical preaching." The topic being set, he must search for a text to fit. Every time he has the uneasy feeling that, in this kind of sermon preparation, he is less responsible to the Word. The lectionary forces him to listen before he determines what he is to say.

The line around evangelicalism is not easy to define. This difference in interpretation of the "unchanging Gospel" is characteristic. It is subtle. In part it is a matter of style, but there is some significant substance behind it all.

F undamentalists seek actively to separate themselves from the culture around themselves ("the world"). Most look backward to the New Testament age, and forward to the "end times." God intervened in history dramatically and decisively in the person of Christ and through the apostles. God will intervene again, even more dramatically. What lies between these two ages counts for little. For some it is merely the backdrop before which the "signs of the times" cross the stage.

They see the "social Gospel"—any attempt to improve society, particularly any left-appearing attempt—as arrogance, as futility, or as heresy, departures characteristic of "modernism." Most evangelicals look instead for "a new heaven and a new earth," (Revelation 21:1) not of their making. They see little that they can do either to quicken it or retard it. It will come in God's own time.

There is, therefore, no special need to understand or come to terms with current society, and no need to speak to it. When they invite, in Jesus' name, a person to come into new life, they invite him or her to come *out* of society.

There is a deep ambiguity in this thinking, however. The disengagement from culture and society seems to have five peculiar exceptions:
• involvement in politics,
• the use of high technology,
• reliance on parachurch organizations,
• a craving for glamor and sensationalism,
• and an ostentatious biblicism.
Though these too are tendencies, they are immensely important ones. They suggest that evangelicalism is as much a culture as a theology.

Recent elections in the United States have shown the close connection of a large part of evangelicalism with the "new right." That generally right-wing political commitment is rooted in the civil involvement of the churches in a past where issues like drunkenness topped the agenda in many places, in classical evangelical readings of God's favor to Israel as a call to "patriotism," in secular biblicism, and in reaction to the "social gospel."

In Canada evangelical involvement in politics is less blatant, and more thoughtful. This is a basic difference within evangelicalism between the two countries.

Years ago, in Calvary Baptist Church, an "end-times lecturer" conducted a series of talks every night for a week or so. He had sewn together five double bedsheets and on them painted, rather amateurishly, a chart of the seven dispensations from creation to the consummation of all things. Thumbtacked to the side wall, his chart extended almost the length of the church. There was so much detail that it was difficult to read, but each night he would explain a section of it.

There is nothing like that at Calvary Baptist Church, today. Instead, they use multimedia presentations of high professional quality.

When Calvary built its new building, it installed state-of-the-art equipment: the best sound system in town, a gigantic rear-projection screen above the baptistry and behind the pulpit, and TV screens in every room. Press a button in the pulpit and a picture—filmstrip, slide, or video—appears. Press another button at the organ and the words to a hymn or chorus take its place. Flip a few switches and all the proceedings are heard and seen in the Sunday School auditorium in full high fidelity.

Invisible from the pews, but with a full view of the pulpit, organ and choir, is a fully equipped recording studio controlling hidden cameras. Every service is recorded. Calvary has a full-time technician on the staff—listed as "minister of electronics" right along with the minister, minister of Christian education, and minister of music. Members can take home audio cassettes or video tapes. The tapes go automatically to shut-ins in the congregation.

Children are brought in from every part of town and the surrounding countryside, but in no ordinary buses. Each bus has its own mobile sound system. It goes out with not just a driver, but also a person specially trained in "bus ministry." Every minute on the road counts for "evangelism."

On the roof of Calvary's new building sits a monstrous dish pointed at a satellite up there somewhere. Bible lessons come in on a regular schedule, taught by professionals, fully supported by the necessary

production crew. Each month United Parcel Service delivers a package of beautifully printed lesson booklets, a copious leader's guide, and usually some posters or other materials to go with the televised lessons. That satellite program goes to many fundamental Baptist churches in every sort of community all across North America. It is used exactly as it is broadcast—there is no possibility of modifying it. That is no problem. Springfield Baptist has checked carefully and found the producers absolutely sound. The congregation can trust what comes from them as fitting exactly with their doctrinal stand, and as being of outstanding technical quality. What more could they ask?

By contrast, the Christian Education Committee at Central United spends hours sorting through curriculum materials. They pick and choose, they modify and adapt, and they innovate. They agonize over what combination will best suit *their* children in the Springfield they know. They would like to use a filmstrip or something like that occasionally, but it is difficult to find a suitable one and work it into their lesson plan. Besides, the filmstrip projector chronically jams.

Any mainline church in Springfield could install high-tech equipment comparable to Calvary's. Practically, few would judge such facilities worth either the initial expense or the running costs. For one thing, there is available a much wider selection of audio-visual materials for use in evangelical churches than in others. Some other churches would find it difficult to keep all that equipment properly fed.

More significantly, however, the mainline churches are uncomfortable with such concentration on technology. It does not seem to fit with their understanding of the church and its task.

Lighthouse Bible Church has much the same uneasiness. They fear that such fascination with technology will sooner or later lead to a drop in doctrinal vigilance. They have seen no trouble yet at Calvary. But they are deeply disturbed about some TV evangelism.

Eagle Wings Christian Book Store opened just five years ago. It hasn't been an easy five years, but it is finally providing a reasonable living for its proprietor, Edna Thompson. She has always thought of her store more as a mission than a business. Six days a week it is the most visible evangelical witness in town, and Edna is proud of that.

She gets most of her books from evangelical publishers, who also see a mission in their business. There are so many evangelical books coming out that she has a hard time selecting. Her customers, however, drop in to chat and tell her how they liked their recent purchases and make suggestions, which helps a lot. They keep her posted on what goes on in the churches too, and sometimes she can stock something that just fits in. Sometimes those special

items make a good profit; if not, they still provide a service.

Eagle Wings is the only place in Springfield to buy Bibles. Mrs. Thompson also carries a few concordances and Bible study books. The latest devotional books and faith-building books by well-known evangelicals are featured much the way "bestsellers" are elsewhere. An occasional thriller—usually based on the Apocalypse—sells almost as well as the popular sex-and-seduction novels at the drugstore.

It's not all religious. Along with the Bible story books Mrs. Thompson carries other children's books. Cookbooks are good steady sellers that help a lot with the cash flow, as do books about "parenting."

She also has a few gifts: mugs inscribed with Bible verses, pendant crosses, religious pictures, creche figures through the late fall... And cards, of course. Just about everybody in Springfield goes there if an elderly aunt has a birthday coming up; for others the drugstore will do. She sold out of retirement cards the week before the Presbyterian pastor's last service.

Word has gotten around that Eagle Wings also carries cards for first communion and confirmation. She doesn't advertise them, but they are there. Fr. Steinbrenner is building up interest in Bible study at St. Patrick's. He sends his parishioners to Eagle Wings. If they ask, Mrs. Thompson points out the "Catholic Bibles" at the end of the bottom shelf—they have an imprimatur. Many buy whichever style and binding they like even if it is "Protestant." Fr. Steinbrenner doesn't care; he says they're all the same Bible anyway.

She even carries a few specifically United Church items, even though they don't sell very well. Evangelicals buy more books—more religious books anyway. The United Church people probably do a little better by the drugstore.

W esley Chalmers usually buys his books in the city at a denominational bookstore. They are mostly the sort that only he, of the Springfield population, would want. Eagle Wings can't afford to stock them. When he started building his library, almost every volume was definitely Protestant and definitely mainline. Now he notices that an increasing number have Catholic authorship, many of them published by non-Catholic presses. He just bought *The New Jerome Biblical Commentary*. It is edited by three Roman Catholic priests, two of them professors at Protestant seminaries.

An increasing number of the books Chalmers buys come from evangelical publishers or evangelical writers. Sometimes it is a little hard to tell; scholarly evangelical publications are not as distinctive as they used to be. If they are good, he figures, why worry about who wrote them?

G. Whitefield Finney buys his books in the city too—at a "Christian book store" several times bigger than Eagle Wings. He is careful to buy only things from sound evangelical sources. Unknown to each other, both have recently bought *Word Biblical Commentary* on John. Finney has long known Word Books as a sound evangelical publisher, but this is a little different from anything he had read before. As he has gotten into it, it has made him a little uneasy. Chalmers finds it an interesting balance for his other commentaries on John. Something is happening in the world of publishing that is a little like the broadening clientele and stock at Eagle Wings.

E agle Wings and the evangelical publishers are both examples of parachurch enterprises, businesses with a mission. There are many: recording studios and music publishers, software houses (the Bible on disk for home computers), choir-gown manufacturers, church-management consultants, builders, you name it. Many of them offer excellent service. Many are also successful commercially.

Though privately owned, many evangelicals think of them as "ours," somehow a little different from the average run of businesses. They help to give evangelicals an identity and to hold them together.

Many more parachurch organizations are non-commercial. They

provide functions that in the mainline churches are taken care of by denominational agencies or inter-church cooperative agencies.

Typically, these organizations are accountable to no superior body, only to the individuals and local churches that support them. That is what is meant by "parachurch." The commercial ones put their product before the evangelical public; that public judges them by *both* commercial and evangelical standards. In most cases that works. It demands, however, that a large part of the constituency must be well informed, fair-minded, and critical.

Edna Thompson's personal faith and conduct counts heavily with the customers at Eagle Wings Christian Book Store. I have been favorably impressed, talking with her, and am sure that the public confidence is well placed. This high valuing of personal charisma, however, presents marvelous opportunities for con artists. Evangelical parachurch organizations have attracted many.

Church bodies exercise oversight over their agencies. This too can fail, of course, but it fails in other ways. Here, the flamboyant con artist has less of a chance. The greater danger is the bureaucratic paper-shuffler.

The non-commercial organizations put a lot of effort into reporting to their constituency. They provide a flood of printed documents and personal letters. They maintain representatives on the road. The supporting public wants evidences of results—clear, specific, testable evidences; the parachurch organizations give it to them.

With it all go assurances that their teaching is evangelical and all personnel are theologically sound. That is crucial. Many of these parachurch organizations have statements of faith, all covering pretty much the same topics. They all make strong affirmations on a narrow list of points.

Mainline churches too have "Statements of Faith," or "Articles of Religion," seldom so conspicuously displayed. These tend to address a much broader range of topics. For example, most have articles on sacraments; evangelical statements seldom do.

A half-page ad in the *Springfield Clarion* announces the annual mission conference at Calvary Baptist Church. Four missionaries will be present. The ad shows a picture of each, with a few tantalizing words of biography. The church supports a dozen missionaries in all. Every one of them has appeared in person in Springfield at least once. A bulletin board in the church exhibits personally written letters from all of them; fresh letters appear almost weekly. Actually, each missionary is shared with at least one other church, so the church is not raising twelve full salaries and associated costs. Nevertheless, the dollar figure is impressive. Calvary Church is strongly committed to overseas missions.

Those twelve missionaries work under six different organizations. Not one of them has the word "Baptist" in its name. One specializes in radio evangelization; another in Bible translation; the other four organizations are more general, each concentrating on some geographical area in the third world. They are all parachurch organizations run by self-perpetuating boards, all explicitly committed to inerrancy. Calvary has satisfied itself that all are sound on every vital point.

The mainline churches in Springfield all support missions too. Their money goes to their denominational mission board. None of it is earmarked for any specific missionary or even a specific field. The people simply assume that it will all be spent in line with the denomination's beliefs and objectives. If the board has a statement of faith, the churches haven't seen it.

There is regular reporting too. Most of it comes in periodicals portraying the work of the church as a whole. Only in special situations do missionaries send personal letters to specific churches. When a missionary comes to visit—not as common an event as in evangelical churches—he or she tries to represent the whole enterprise. Little will be said about the needs of that particular missionary.

All the names in the *Clarion* ad are familiar to the Calvary Baptist people. For many of them so are the faces. The accompanying statements are intended to entice some hearers from outside the membership. There are other attractions, too. Special music will be by "The Hallelujah Chorus," billed as "one of the most thrilling Gospel groups of recent times, just returned from a triumphant tour through nine countries! Come early to be sure of a seat!"

The turnout for this particular mission conference was a bit larger than usual. Those missionaries had exciting stories, excellent pictures— effectively shown on that large screen—and some interesting souvenirs from the field. The high point was a surprise announcement that one of Calvary's own members had just been accepted for service in Papua-

New Guinea. The missions committee recommended that Calvary Baptist support her. The collections were large, and pledges even larger.

Calvary Baptist's weekly ad is usually as large as all the mainline churches' ads together. Always there is something sensational. The pastor's own sermon titles are as punchy as he can make them. Visiting preachers get star treatment. One ad announced a "World-renowned student of prophecy" preaching on "Perestroika—has it changed the timetable?" Another proclaimed "Free at last" by "a convict converted on death row and miraculously pardoned by prayer." Both with photographs, of course—one a prison mug shot.

There seems to be special appeal for some evangelical churches in dramatic conversion from an extraordinarily sinful past: drug pushers, street-gang leaders, bank robbers, shady politicians, all miraculously converted and ready to tell all about their sordid life before and their glorious life after. The implication is clear: "If God can save such desperately evil people, God can certainly save me, tainted only by much more minor sins." For some reason, I have never seen reborn sexual perverts or child abusers on that preaching circuit. Is it that God can only change some kinds, or that the audiences impose some limits on what they want to hear?

Most of these people are busy going around a circuit of churches. The most successful of them—the ones booked into the biggest churches—are supported by all the necessary staff for a touring Nashville celebrity. Their fees are proportional.

Calvary Baptist Church doesn't get the top names, but you would never know that from the hype in the ads. It doesn't have to settle for the bottom of the list either. Mid-range celebrities like to go there because of the great acoustics, the fine sound system, and the tremendous effort put into getting an audience. Having a good overflow crowd in the Sunday School auditorium is great. The next place will be able to advertise "preaches everywhere to overflow crowds."

Lighthouse Bible Church does occasionally have visiting preachers or singing groups (most often the choir from some nearby sister church). Finney and his board are much more interested in getting ones who will make a solid contribution. They put a special ad in the *Clarion*, but with much less hype. The speakers I have heard were not quite as smooth talkers as either that "world-renowned prophecy lecturer" or that "convict from death row," but I thought both had more thoughtful messages. One Calvary Baptist revival was conducted by a preacher who had "converted a thousand precious souls in one service." Finney carefully picked as his text that Sunday: "I have planted, Apollos watered; but God gave the increase." (1 Corinthians 3:6) He didn't say a word about the ad. Nor did he explicitly criticize evangelism by numbers. He didn't have to. Almost everyone had seen at least the posters on the telephone poles all over tøwn, or in the window at Eagle Wings. The people understood, and most went right along with him. They want him to preach the truth in love. They don't want to get ensnared in the world's judgment of success.

When Central United has a guest speaker, it rarely provides more publicity than the speaker's name on the bulletin board on the front lawn. The turnout that Sunday is often smaller than when Wesley Chalmers speaks. The church members know and trust Chalmers; he is their pastor. They rarely know—or care much about—the visitor.

Perhaps the most telling difference between the "evangelical" and "mainline" churches is in the way they handle (literally) the Bible. In the mainline churches it is a book, physically little different from other books, however special its contents may be. For many "evangelicals" the actual volume has special values.

"Christian book stores" predictably feature Bibles. One I have patronized several times has them in a central display, straight ahead as you enter the store. The floor is raised a step or two; the area is carpeted, there is a tasteful oak railing, and a couple of easy chairs for browsers. The Bibles themselves are displayed on expensive-looking oak shelving. Elsewhere in the store, there are good, standard commercial fixtures.

Most evangelical churches have a Bible open on the pulpit. Yet no preacher will walk in without another in his hand. There are Bibles in the pews, yet every member brings one along. Any evangelical gathering bristles with Bibles.

When the actual book is not present, there are often reminders: I have seen a car bearing the vanity plate "JN 316". Biblical bumper stickers and T-shirts abound.

The Bible has become for many more than an "infallible [or inerrant] guide to faith and practice." Perhaps it is a totem.

COMMUNICATION FAILURE

Zachariah Elliott enjoys the best of terms with his neighbor Kenneth Moore. They have a lot in common; they both enjoy hunting and fishing. Ken has been to Zack's cottage a couple of times in deer season. They bowl in the same league every Wednesday. They worked together to establish the Little League and are still deeply involved. The two families went to Disney World together.

They are both active in their churches. Zack is the Sunday School superintendent at Lighthouse Bible Church and Ken is on the board at Central United Church. They talk about everything else, but they seldom discuss church or religion. That's too bad; each could learn something from the other.

Of course, they would disagree on a number of points, and they know that. However, they argue passionately about baseball, football, and hockey, where they support competing big league teams and have different visions for the sports. So the problem is not just differences of opinion. It seems to be more that they don't understand each other. It's a bit like one person talking baseball while the other was talking hockey— no, more like cricket and jai alai, where one talker is English and the other Mexican.

The fact is, when they talk religion, Ken doesn't have the foggiest idea what Zack is saying half the time, and vice versa. With baseball, they at least know what they're disagreeing about.

Ken Moore's neighbor on the other side is Seiji Takahashi. They too have a great deal in common, both being industrial engineers. They have always been on good terms, and Ken would really like to get better acquainted. Yet he finds it somehow difficult to talk with him beyond the simplest formal exchanges.

It is not a simple matter of language. Seiji Takahashi came to Springfield already quite competent in English, and by now he is fluent, with only a touch of an accent. When they have business dealings— Moore's firm supplies some of the plastic for Takahashi's gearshift-knob plant—there is no difficulty whatever.

But in social matters the two operate on different wavelengths. Each of them has the same feeling: You never are quite sure what is going on.

It's uncomfortable. Without trying to analyze it in detail, we can say the problem is "cultural."

Takahashi San doesn't even know how to talk about the weather. He knows all the meteorological vocabulary—"altostratus," "occluded front"—but, when someone asks, "Hot enough for you?" he takes it as a serious question. After several efforts—perhaps involving some very precise observations about "thermal inversions"—he has gotten wary of casual questions. Those who know him have learned not to ask.

It is the same problem between Ken and Zack, except it arises only with religion. They share all the conventions when it comes to talking about sports, or politics, or community affairs...but not religion. Vocabulary differences are just the beginning; the biggest problems are cultural: different ways of using their different vocabularies, different social conventions as to what you talk about, when, and at what level. Moore has the same uncomfortable feeling talking with Takahashi about almost anything except plastic resins.

Pastor Finney and Rev. Chalmers have the same problem—with one difference. Both being professional ministers, it is a little harder to settle down the way Elliott and Moore have, talking freely about everything *except* religion. Besides, Finney and Chalmers have never lived next door to each other.

Ken Moore and Zack Elliott are not unique. There are many similar pairs, not just in Springfield, but almost anywhere in North America. There are, however, others with similarly diverse backgrounds—though possibly not as good friends—who do occasionally discuss religion.

When they do talk religion, there is one thing you can bet on. It will only be a few minutes before the matter of biblical authority comes up. And the odds are better than nine to one that it will be the "evangelical" who raises it. Chances are, too, that the "mainliner" will be uncomfortable when it does come up.

Exactly how the matter is raised may vary. Something may be said about the "authority of the Bible," or about "trusting God's Word," or "The Bible says," or "as St. Paul said..." or it may be nothing more than the introduction of a Bible verse, quoted without explanation and with an air of finality, as if to indicate, "That's it, there's nothing more to say."

There is a good chance the non-evangelical isn't intimately acquainted with that particular verse anyway. Even if he or she is, what does one do next? It seems a little boorish to respond with "So what?" or to flatly contradict the Bible, or to ask "What has that got to do with this matter?" or to just go on as if nothing has been said.

Do you remember that plaque on Pastor Finney's wall: "Go ye." The Lighthouse members who see it all know what it means:

Go ye into all the world, and preach the Gospel to every creature. He that believeth and is baptized shall be saved. (Mark 16:15b–16a)

If you don't have that quotation stored away in your memory somewhere, that slogan will be meaningless. As a matter of fact, you have to have not just the verse, but an agreed interpretation of it. Most of the people coming into Finney's office have that background.

That verse is a prooftext. It is special only because it is commonly shortened into a two-word slogan. Otherwise it works just like many, many others.

Prooftexts of the garden variety call up a great deal of commonly held, stored information. People like the members of Lighthouse use them, primarily, to keep each other reminded of common convictions. Sometimes they summarize what has been said so far, consolidating everything in preparation for the next step in the discussion.

Even when they are used—as they sometimes are—to score a point or to start the discussion off in another direction, they depend on shared understanding. That shared understanding might come from sitting, Sunday after Sunday, in Lighthouse Bible Church, where many useful texts are quoted time after time. Or sitting under Brother Amos Finney in his little unfinished Love One Another Tabernacle. Or, for that matter, listening regularly to certain radio or TV preachers. All these make heavy use of a characteristic selection of prooftexts. Since it is people with a broadly common background who share this knowledge, prooftexts also signal membership in the in-group.

Rev. Wesley Chalmers does a lot less of that sort of repetitive quoting. Even if he did, the verses would be different; the interpretation would be different too. His preaching does not provide a base for communication with those using this selection of prooftexts.

So, when Zack Elliott uses familiar prooftexts in speaking to Ken Moore, they cannot possibly work as he intends. Elliott does not understand that his prooftexts are in-group devices. He does not realize how limited they are when addressed to outsiders. Elliott is accustomed to using prooftexts in certain conventional ways in certain contexts. In those situations, he simply does not know how to talk to non-prooftexters.

There is a similar difficulty the other way. Elliott expects a certain kind of religious discourse to contain prooftexts. He relies on them to keep track of where the discussion is going. Without them he gets a little disoriented. He has trouble following the logical development in Ken Moore's arguments about religion.

Ken Moore, of course, has the opposite set of difficulties. He doesn't know how to use prooftexts—and doesn't have a stock of them to use in any case. He realizes that Zack is not getting the full message, but he has little idea of what the problem is.

After a few experiences of talking past each other, they concluded (subconsciously perhaps) that it wasn't worth straining their otherwise good relationship.

P rooftexts are not the only way Bible verses are quoted. Go into any fairly large "Christian book store" and you will find many volumes dealing with broadly theological topics. Pick one of the more scholarly looking ones and open it at random; you will almost certainly find a verse or two right there on the page before you. They may be familiar (to the regular readers of that sort of literature) or they may not. Either way, they will be carefully related to one another. Something may be said about the context out of which they come.

Go into a seminary library and seek out comparable works from deep within Academia. You will find very much the same thing—except that the passages may be quoted in Greek or Hebrew.

What you are seeing is the marshalling of evidence to support a scholarly point. One was written for well-informed lay evangelicals; the other for the writer's colleagues and for the most scholarly of clergy, like Chalmers. In many ways the scholarship in the two books is quite different, but in each case you can have confidence that the author has examined all the evidence judged relevant, and has carefully selected the phrases, verses, or longer passages quoted in the book. They have not been pulled out of a little anthology of familiar verses, each with its own standard meaning and function. Rather they have been selected directly from the Bible and closely considered in their original context.

We often call both sorts of Bible passages "prooftexts," but they are significantly different. Garden variety prooftexts carry a great deal of special meaning put into them by conventional use. Scholarly quotations from the Bible carry much less of this baggage.

B ible verses acquire special meaning and special uses, making them prooftexts. That happens more commonly in churches like Lighthouse, so that we think of prooftexts as characteristic of fundamentalist churches. The same thing happens, however, with single words in all segments of the church. This is less often noticed, but is an even more serious obstacle to communication.

"Blood" has come up frequently in our description of Lighthouse. It is a favorite word there, frequently used in preaching and in any discussion around some of the cardinal doctrines of the church.

Central avoids the word except at communion, when the traditional, biblical words are used: "This Cup is the new covenant in my Blood..." and "The Blood of our Lord Jesus Christ which was shed for you..." Communion is very meaningful to many in the United Churches, and these words carry part of the meaning. "Blood" has acquired a special connection with communion, so special that it seems a little out of place in any other context. It does not bring to mind the meanings that Lighthouse hears in "blood."

Much of the meaning of "blood" at Lighthouse rests on what is called "typology," the conviction that many of the themes of the Old Testament are "types" or foreshadowings of New Testament themes.

A great deal of the Old Testament deals with sacrifices. Much of the book of Leviticus is devoted to specifying when and how the sacrifices are to be performed. In all this, the blood is special. Christ's death on the cross, the central event in the New Testament, is seen as a sacrifice. So the Old Testament sacrificial system is a type, a foreshadowing of the crucifixion. Each gives insight into the other, and each must be interpreted in the light of the other. Always the New Testament is the heart of the matter; the earlier system is a foreshadowing.

Typology is no modern invention, though it has been greatly elaborated in recent times. It is the basis for a great deal of the New Testament Letter to the Hebrews, particularly in chapters 9 and 10. The following four verses give the heart of the argument:

> But when Christ appeared as a high priest of the good things that have come, then through the greater and more perfect tabernacle (not made with hands, that is, not of this creation) he entered once for all in the Holy Place, taking not the blood of goats and calves but his own blood, thus securing an eternal redemption. For if the sprinkling of defiled persons with the blood of goats and bulls and with the ashes of a heifer sanctifies for the purification of the flesh, how much more shall the blood of Christ, who through the eternal Spirit offered himself without blemish to God, purify your conscience from dead works to serve the living God. (Hebrews 9:11–14 RSV)

Finney greatly values this passage, not only for what it proclaims as Gospel, but also as a model for the use of the Old Testament in preaching and in the establishment of doctrine.

Chalmers, like most of his colleagues in the United Church, rarely uses typology in Bible interpretation. Indeed, he rarely uses Hebrews (except chapter 11) in his preaching or teaching. (One merit of the lectionary is it forces preachers at least to read parts of these chapters.) Similarly, Chalmers tends to avoid other briefer mentions of the "blood" of Christ, such as:

> Since, therefore, we are now justified by his blood, much more shall we be saved by him from the wrath of God. (Romans 5:9 RSV)
> In him we have redemption through his blood, the forgiveness of our trespasses, according to the riches of his grace. (Ephesians 1:7 RSV)

Chalmers does not avoid all such passages. For example, he likes this one:

> And they sung a new song, saying, Thou art worthy to take the book, and to open the seals thereof: for thou wast slain, and hast redeemed us to God, by thy blood out of every kindred, and tongue, and people, and nation. (Revelation 5:9 KJV)

The two preachers choose different themes when they preach on this passage, though. Chalmers always emphasizes "out of every kindred and tongue and people and nation." He considers it one of the great texts for the universality of the Gospel. Finney does not neglect these words, but focuses on "hast redeemed us to God, by thy blood."

V erses like those give "blood" a great deal of meaning for the people at Lighthouse. When they see that others make less of it, "blood" acquires for them additional meanings, making it a symbol of their own identity as a faithful people.

When my son was in high school, I sometimes asked him about slang that I heard. Frequently he would answer with something like, "That's a Kingswood word, not a Watkinson word." Watkinson was his school; some of his friends went to Kingswood. Slang and church jargon are alike in this: they always carry this second kind of meaning.

That is a potent factor in communication failure. We feel uncomfortable with words or phrases we suspect of carrying special symbolic meaning for another group.

P rooftexts and specially loaded vocabulary are just two obstacles to communication. Basic assumptions, often unstated, pose difficulties too.

For Zachariah Elliott a strong commitment to the authority of the Bible undergirds all that he says. That must be understood, if his words are to be properly interpreted. It remains true even if he says nothing directly about that authority, even if he is not speaking about the Bible at all.

Sooner or later, in any conversation between a fundamentalist and a mainliner, there will be some more explicit formulation of a doctrine of authority. The word "inerrant," or "inerrancy," or something related will appear. Like "blood" these words have both denotations and connotations—simple meanings and emotional overtones. Between the evangelicals and mainliners both kinds of meaning will be different.

These words generally summarize a conviction that every statement made in the Bible, on any subject, must be true. It goes along with an assumption that any question can have only one true answer, and, therefore, there can be no contradiction or discrepancy in the Bible.

That meaning might, or might not, occur to a person like Ken Moore the first time "inerrancy" came up. It is very unlikely that all the implications would be clear. In any case, the implications extend far beyond the simple meaning.

For the people at Lighthouse, and at thousands of evangelical churches, inerrancy is a pivotal doctrine. Everything hangs on it. It motivates much of what they do; it is why they read the Bible in worship services, why the preaching is Bible-based, why the educational program of the church is devoted either to teaching the Bible or to teaching doctrines directly from the Bible. Ultimately it is why Lighthouse Bible Church takes that name, perhaps even why the church exists. Lighthouse members expect inerrancy to underlie the practices of other churches. They can imagine no workable alternative. They are genuinely puzzled that other churches can preach from the Bible without accepting it as inerrant.

For the people at Central United and in thousands of other churches, no doctrine about the Bible has that same kind of centrality. For them, the Bible has a key place because it speaks of Christ. Christ is the basis of their faith; the Bible has a secondary, but still very high, importance.

Central's members are generally not very clear in this matter. You have to push them a bit to get any precise statement of the sort, and you may never get it from some. Yet it is certainly their experience. They have heard a great deal more preaching about Christ than they have about the Bible. That preaching has always been Bible-based. Consequently, they are accustomed to the Bible as a way to hear about Christ.

If you put the question to them just right, some might say that the Bible speaks reliably about Christ. That is enough to give it a dominant place in their services of worship and in preaching.

People at Central are puzzled by the doctrine of inerrancy. It seems to put the emphasis in the wrong place. It seems to stress that the Bible is true in all sorts of minor details: the precise age of Methuselah, the succession of petty kings in Israel, the genealogies...as if only the details matter.

A few have heard a debate, probably involving at least one inerrantist, about how many of each animal went into Noah's ark. One account says two of each; another says two of some and seven of others. Such a debate will generate some pretty fancy footwork to reconcile the two accounts. That sort of treatment seems to push the Bible story toward a kind of trivialization that the members of Central find distasteful.

This is nothing new. Back in old Springfield Henry Withers, the free-thinker, loved to ask "If Adam and Eve had only two boys, as the Bible says, where did they get their wives?" Some people got very upset by this—precisely what Henry intended. Most simply laughed it off as a joke. The inerrantist seems to be in the heritage of those whom Henry

Withers could annoy with a stock of similar questions. None of them addressed any point that really seemed to matter.

Most sports fans have hobby issues that they ride mercilessly. Zack Elliott's is league expansion. He can give 99 reasons for franchising six more major-league baseball teams. He thinks he has a good answer to every objection that anyone could possibly raise. He and Ken Moore have argued this point many times.

Zack has encountered a variety of opposing opinions. Ken argues that the present set-up is near ideal; expansion would bring more troubles than benefits. A mutual friend maintains that the present troubles in baseball are a direct result of expansion; we need to get back to the old six-team leagues. (He also thinks the Dodgers should still be in Brooklyn.) Another agrees that more teams would be great, but not in the present two leagues; there should be a third major league. And Atanasio Romero, who coaches in the Little League has his own idea. "I'll go for four more teams, but only if they are in San Juan, San Pedro de Macaris, Caracas, and Mexico City."

Zack has learned one thing for certain: opposing his idea of expansion does not automatically mean favoring the present setup.

Zack's mind works differently on inerrancy: if you don't accept his idea of the Bible, you don't accept the Bible at all. The only possible other position is one he calls "errancy"—he got that term from sermons at Lighthouse Bible Church, but it was not original there. If the Bible is not true everywhere, it must be in error someplace. If it is in error any place, how can you trust it?

The usual tactic is to ask something like, "You don't believe in inerrancy, so give me one place where the Bible is wrong." At best, that makes the other person a little uncomfortable; it's not the way one would choose to approach the problem. Ken doesn't want to get into that again.

Zack thinks Ken is all wrong about baseball expansion, but he understands his position. He does not understand his friend's position on the Bible. He has never gotten any satisfactory answer when in desperation he has asked, "OK, you don't believe in inerrancy and you don't believe in errancy, so what do you believe in?"

Zack Elliott has a problem here: he sees the question simply as black or white. He shares that problem with many others. Ken Moore, however, has a problem too, shared just as widely: he doesn't know how to express his position. Perhaps, if he could present an alternative, he might have led his friend a little toward looking at religion differently—more like the way he looks at league expansion. Moore's problem is not his personally. Central United Church has never given Moore a clear *verbal statement* that he can fall back on. What Moore and the other members of Central have picked up has come mainly from example. The Scripture has been read every Sunday; Chalmers and his predecessors have labored valiantly to clarify it and make it apply to life in Springfield. They evidently feel the Bible has something unique to say to people—today's people in today's world. Central United Church members like that way of doing things. They accept the Bible as pivotal, the same way Chalmers does. They consider themselves to be a small fragment of Christ's church, so Christ comes first for them—in their church life anyway (and they'd like to be more faithful on weekdays too). The Bible comes right behind, as the book that tells them of Christ.

Communication failure between churches and church members is nothing new.

Think of all those Irish Catholic maids in old Springfield. Each got fairly well acquainted with an old-family evangelical housewife. They talked every day, generally successfully, about cleaning and washing and ironing and cooking and all the other household operations. They at least tried to talk about other things. The employer might be genuinely interested in the employee's family. She would share the grief over deaths and the joy at births, baptisms, and marriages. The Irish maid would do the same.

When first communions and confirmations came along, the evangelical would understand the joy, but not the occasion for it. Conversely, the annual revival would come along, and one of the young people in the family would make a personal confession of faith. The maid would understand something of the joy, but almost nothing of the reason for it.

Always there would be some communication problem, great or small. Some evangelicals simply gave up. It seemed hopeless to discuss such matters.

But an occasional employer, being a convinced evangelical, and concerned for the other, would attempt to "lead her to Christ." At this point the failure to communicate could be extreme, and the experience most unsatisfactory, perhaps even traumatic, for both of them. Except for the barrel factory, all the businesses in Springfield were small. The boss was always a member of one of the evangelical churches. The janitor, the drayman, or some other employee was likely to be Irish and Catholic. There was the same personal contact that the women had, and the same limits on communication. They understood each other on some matters, but when religion came up—as it did from time to time— almost invariably something was not understood, or totally misunderstood.

Springfield's evangelical churches and their members were not strong on church history—beyond the close of Acts, anyway. They did know, however vaguely they placed it in context, of Luther standing firm for his principles and confronting the Church of Rome with the Bible. It was always "the Bible against Rome" and "Rome against the Bible." That gave them a way to explain to themselves all these puzzling, frustrating, and enigmatic interchanges with their Catholic workers: Catholics were simply not Bible-reading, evangelical Christians, and therefore hardly Christians at all. For many Springfield people, experience amply confirmed this verdict.

The Irish Catholics, for their part, had a long-standing experience with Protestants in the old country. It had not been good. That gave them their way to understand. They also had well-established personal and communal defenses against Protestantism. Fr. Ryan shared them, of course, and saw it as part of his priestly duty to keep them strong.

It was different only in detail with the Lutherans. They did have a great deal more in common with the evangelicals than did the Irish Catholics. However, they worshiped in German, had learned catechism in German, prayed in German, and were ill-at-ease talking religion in English.

Even if, by some stroke of luck, they had acquired English religious vocabulary there was much more that they needed to know. It included all that cultural baggage. That extra was not easy to learn.

All the same frustrations and embarrassments of evangelical-Catholic contacts could and did arise. If the English-speaking people had thought of them as Lutherans they might still have been puzzled. Lutherans ought to stand with Luther, and that should make them evangelicals too, pretty much like the rest. It did not occur to the Springfield evangelicals that perhaps their picture of Luther was partial and a bit distorted.

In any case, the Springfield elite did not think of them as Lutherans so much as Germans. That covered up for them this possible point of contact. Germans were different, more different than most people knew how to cope with. What is strange is always seen as difficult.

"Stereotype" has not occurred in the last dozen paragraphs, but it labels what these paragraphs describe. We may not like to recognize the fact, but new intergroup contacts always result in stereotypes. Some are relatively benign, but some are not. It takes time, effort, and patience to replace the worst ones with less harmful, and to work toward a more ideal relationship.

It would take only a generation or so for the evangelicals to start accepting Lutherans not merely as outsiders but as fellows. It only took a generation or so more for them to be fully accepted in some areas.

With the Roman Catholics it took a lot longer. There were old animosities on both sides, and they were deeply ingrained. Antagonism was institutionalized. In Central Canada one of the chief social forces was the Orange Order, its ideology rooted in the Catholic-Protestant conflicts in Ireland. Every July 12 they held a parade, occasionally going out of their way to annoy the Catholics. Every St. Patrick's day they were on hand to see if the parade could not be converted into a melee.

In the United States, the situation was no less nasty, coming up for a while in the "Know Nothings," and at a later date in the Ku Klux Klan, and along the way in various other forms.

In all of it, the biggest element was communication failure, both the lack of means and the limitation of will.

THE CHANGING BIBLE

Fifty years ago, in communities like Springfield, everyone was familiar with the Bible. It came in three common varieties:

One: A book, moderate in size though containing over a thousand pages, printed on a special kind of paper ("Bible paper") very seldom used in any other book. The pages were usually edged in gold. It was almost always bound in a peculiar sort of limp black leather binding and stamped in gold "HOLY BIBLE." Typical examples were at least moderately worn from being carried back and forth to church and from frequent reading. Such can conveniently be labelled "personal Bibles." Every church member was expected to own one, and most did, as did many non-members. Receiving their first Bible was an event for many children.

Two: A somewhat larger book, generally displayed on a table in the front room, commonly known as the "family Bible." It often had an elaborately tooled padded leather cover with gold stamping. Its defining feature was a set of special pages, provided for keeping records of major events in the family. Here were listed births, marriages, and deaths for the household and relatives. There were often a few related clippings or photographs tucked in.

Three: A book about the size of the largest family Bibles, but without any of those special record pages. It lay permanently open on the pulpit—or, in the occasional church that made a distinction, on the lectern—with ribbons hanging out. It was known as a "pulpit Bible." From it were read the lessons each Sunday, though many pastors found it more convenient to read them from a smaller personal Bible. (They could mark their chosen passage in the margin; no one would do that in the great pulpit Bible.)

The pages in all three were much alike. The text was almost invariably set in two columns, and broken up into small numbered paragraphs known as verses. Under centered chapter headings were often brief listings of major topics. Between the two text columns, and marked off by fine lines, was a very narrow column giving cross references in tiny type. In most Bibles proper names had hyphens and marks over the vowels to indicate the pronunciation. Many personal Bibles included a few maps in the back and a brief concordance, and perhaps some other helps for readers—a chronology, an index of major texts for important topics, a table of ancient weights and measures. Some had the words of Jesus printed in red. Those peculiar physical features set the Bible off from all other books. Even children could recognize it before they learned to read. Distinctive forms were reinforced by distinctive habitats and distinctive uses—even a distinctive etiquette: many people were careful never to place anything on top of their Bible, for example. It seemed a little strange to go into a public library and find a Bible with a call number on the spine sitting on the shelf just like any other book.

In another sense, "the Bible" referred to the text printed within these books. In this, there was even less difference from one Bible to another. Indeed, even trivial differences could be disturbing. I remember a very distant cousin from the United Kingdom seeing a Bible in my home and discovering that it used American spelling; she told my parents that they should get rid of "that book" and get a proper Bible.

People paid little attention to the title page, which almost invariably read:

The Holy Bible
Containing the Old and New Testaments Translated out of the
Original Tongues and with the former Translations Diligently
Compared and Revised by His Majesty's Special Command.
Authorized King James Version

Few people noticed that long subtitle, and fewer had much idea of what it meant.

Even more thoroughly ignored was the preface. It gave some puzzling explanations about relationships to earlier translations and about the translators' procedures. Most puzzling of all, it seemed to disclaim any perfection in the translation.

Almost all Bibles were, as that title page indicated, the King James Version. For most people that was the only one they knew. Therefore, very seldom was anything said about the translation used. Why bother if they knew no alternative?

Actually, other versions were around. In 1870 a committee was set up in Britain to revise the King James. The result was the Revised Version (New Testament 1881; Old Testament 1885). Despite some initial enthusiasm, the Revised Version never really caught hold. The American Standard Edition of the Revised Version, a minor improvement, appeared in 1901. It too had only limited popular support, but it was commonly recommended for close study in seminary Bible courses. Like the English edition, it was more literal than the King James, even occasionally to the point of unintelligibility.

Very occasionally the American Standard Version, as it was commonly called, appeared in Sunday School classrooms—used mostly by adult classes. This would often be an indication that Bible study was taken particularly seriously in that church. But nobody thought of memorizing passages from it, for example.

Then there were a half dozen "private versions," translated by individuals on their own initiative. Each was known to a limited clientele. In my student circle the hands-down favorite was *The Bible; a New Translation* by James Moffatt. This was different enough in all kinds of peculiar ways to appeal to young rebels and to appall their elders.

The Christian student association at my university, like many other similar organizations, sent out groups of students on weekend "deputations" to churches within easy reach. We would often lead the morning service. Usually we read the Scripture from the Moffatt version—often one of the social-justice passages from Isaiah or Amos. I had a Moffatt Bible in an ordinary book binding that I used in my residence, but I also had one in leather—disguised to look like a "real Bible"—that I used on such occasions. We relished the shock that we sometimes produced, though most congregations were too polite to say much. Anyway, next Sunday their own pastor would take them back to the "real Bible."

Today the language of the King James Bible is commonly said to be unintelligible. It was not so fifty years ago. The language was special, to be sure—but to church people, at least, neither strange nor unknown, merely "biblical." Many Bible passages had been memorized in childhood; memorization is one of the best ways to learn a language or a dialect. Sunday Schools had patiently explained the meanings of enough passages that church people had learned a good deal of this special language from an early age. Particularly knotty verses had been amply commented on.

For example, all my student friends knew something of the history of "let," meaning "prevent," as Paul was said to have used it in Romans 1:13:

Now I would not have you ignorant, brethren, that oftentimes I purposed to come unto you, (but was let hitherto,) that I might have some fruit among you also, even as among other Gentiles.

Compare Moffatt's version:

Brothers, I would like you to understand that I have often purposed to come to you (though up till now I have been prevented), so as to have some results among you as well as among the rest of the Gentiles.

The English of the King James, learned in Sunday School and church, was reinforced in the public schools by the teaching of Shakespeare. Indeed, those who led in public worship learned to speak with a great deal of the King James sort of English mixed in. It was customary in public prayer. Even the students who read the lessons from Moffatt conformed to this practice. No one I knew until well into middle age would think of praying aloud in any other way.

Not until the 1950s was there any noticeable movement away from "thou art" in public prayer. Interestingly, the shift started with fundamentalist or evangelical churches (generally considered "conservative"). Mainline churches (generally considered "liberal" or even "radical") lagged behind at least a decade.

This King James-like language was recognized even beyond the church. It was used occasionally to lend an air of solemnity to any public speaking.

"**K**ing James" English was widely understood. That is not to say that it was always correctly understood. For example, the word "doctrine" has shifted its meaning over the years. Consider two occurrences (the first has several parallels):

And they were astonished at his doctrine: for he taught them as one that had authority, and not as the scribes. (Mark 1:22)

In recent decades this has generally been interpreted as "They were astonished at the content of Jesus' teaching." This tends to make Christ into a theologian. The correct meaning, however, is "they were astonished at the *manner* of Jesus' teaching."

And they continued steadfastly in the apostles' doctrine and fellowship, and in breaking of bread, and in prayers. (Acts 2:42)

This has been taken, especially by evangelicals, as indicating that the new Christians held resolutely to a certain theology which they had gotten from the apostles. In this they were seen as a model for the church today, which must be united in its dogma. The original meaning of the Greek (and of the King James English) is however more like "they continued to listen to the apostles as they taught."

Neither misinterpretation is the result of bad translating. In 1611 "act of teaching" or "manner of teaching" was a perfectly acceptable and even ordinary meaning for "doctrine."

The first new Bible translation in English to seriously challenge the King James was the Revised Standard Version (RSV). The New Testament appeared in 1946. The pastors at Central United, Springfield, and at Trinity, Barnesborough, both bought copies almost immediately and began using it in their sermon preparation. After a bit they began cautiously to quote it in their sermons. The lesson for the day, of course, would still be read from the King James. There seemed to be no particular reaction from either congregation.

The Old Testament appeared in 1952. A storm of controversy followed. Reginald Scott, Chalmers' old Sunday School superintendent, for example, was adamant: "That blasphemous book will never be seen in my Sunday School!" His pastor bought a complete Bible and found the Old Testament quite satisfactory, as he had already found the New. Like many other United Church ministers, he did not quote it publicly until the excitement subsided. Then he found that the people liked the RSV, and he and many others gradually began to read lessons from it.

Reginald Scott's reaction was produced not by the translation itself but by reports in the popular press, always quick to pick up anything sensational. Denunciations were quoted under sensational headlines.

A few people, either out of real concern or because they saw an opportunity to get a little publicity, went all out. There were book burnings and other dramatic condemnations, all generating "news." The newspapers had a field day.

Whether they felt the matter was significant or not, all "conservative" preachers sooner or later had to line up in at least symbolic opposition to the new version. Opposition to the RSV gave a small extra push to the emerging modern evangelical movement. Many people felt that it called for united action to "save the Bible."

The New Revised Standard Version has just appeared. It has further modernized the language and incorporated some new insights. It is too early to say anything about its reception, but we can be sure that there will be far less anguish and agitation than greeted its predecessor in the fifties.

P art of the problem with the RSV was the translation itself. The King James had Isaiah saying:

> Behold, a virgin shall conceive, and bear a son, and shall call his name Immanuel. (Isaiah 7:14)

The RSV had:

> Behold, a young woman shall conceive and bear a son, and shall call his name Immanuel.

The bitter theological controversies of the twenties had not died. The virgin birth was still, for many, the touchstone of orthodoxy. The "liberals," according to the popular stereotype, flatly rejected it. "Young woman" here could be taken as a denial of that doctrine.

It did not matter that the RSV had "virgin" in the more crucial verses in Matthew and Luke. Nor did it matter that the RSV translation did not deny the doctrine; "young woman" is strictly neutral. Nor did it matter that the Hebrew word here clearly meant "young woman" at other places; here, it was insisted, it must mean "virgin." Some of the arguments even pitted the King James against the Hebrew, and in effect argued that the 1611 translation was more reliable than the ancient original.

The argument was bitter, primarily because it forced some people to change their ways of thinking, teaching, and preaching. They could say that they were defending a fundamental doctrine. They were in fact defending an established way of arguing for a doctrine that was not actually threatened.

Some evangelicals opposed the RSV translation on the basis of a carefully thought-out understanding of the relation of the New Testament to the Old, and of the use of the New Testament in interpreting the Old. Their position got less attention than it should have because it was drowned out by the more raucous criticism. The discussion was taken out of the hands of the scholars, and out of the hands of the more rational ministers and lay people, and was put in the hands of rabble-rousers.

Condemnation of the RSV spread beyond the churches into the general public. One very minor incident will illustrate the nature of some of the opposition.

I was visiting a man who had been raised a Methodist, but had not been attending church for many years. He asked me what I thought of the "new Bible." I had been through the controversy before, so I dodged the question by asking him what he thought of it. He was very strongly opposed, because "they had taken out the virgin birth." I asked, "Where?" He paused a minute and then said, somewhat haltingly, "You know, that place that goes 'who was conceived by the Holy Ghost, born of the Virgin Mary, suffered under Pontius Pilate...' They changed that." His memory had confused the Apostle's Creed, frequently used in the church of his youth, with the Bible.

The Bible had thus become a cultural symbol. Our society made its own claim to it. Many of the unchurched felt an obligation to defend the Bible from tinkering by church people. (If this sounds a little reminiscent of attitudes in the days of classical evangelicalism, there is good reason. Not all of the heritage remained within the church.)

Actually the difference between the KJV and the RSV was often not great, particularly in some of the very familiar passages:

KJV	RSV
The Lord is my shepherd;	The Lord is my shepherd,
I shall not want,	I shall not want;
He maketh me to lie down in green pastures:	he makes me lie down in green pastures.
He leadeth me beside the still waters.	He leads me beside still waters;
...	...
Thou preparest a table before me	Thou preparest a table before me
in the presence of mine enemies:	in the presence of my enemies;
thou anointest my head with oil;	thou anointest my head with oil,
my cup runneth over.	my cup overflows.

(I don't know the mind of the committee that produced the RSV, but I suspect that the one major vocabulary change here was simply to preserve a bit of rhythm: "My cup runs over" loses a desirable unstressed syllable. The New Revised Standard Version, 1990, differs only in "You prepare" and "you anoint" instead of "Thou preparest" and "thou anointest.")

The most striking difference between the KJV and the RSV was the appearance of the pages. The RSV printed most of the text in paragraphs, with the verse numbers present but less conspicuous; some (like the psalm quoted) is printed as poetry. The latter change was a shock to some pious people; in populist America, poetry is often seen as verging on the frivolous, inappropriate for anything as serious as the Bible.

More significant changes were harder to notice. Their full extent only gradually came to attention. For example, Psalm 145:13 reads:

KJV	RSV
Thy kingdom is an everlasting kingdom,	Thy kingdom is an everlasting kingdom,
and thy dominion endureth	and thy dominion endures
throughout all generations.	throughout all generations.
——	The Lord is faithful in all his words,
——	and gracious in all his deeds.

In this passage the RSV includes two lines not in the KJV. The committee of translators accepted the judgement of many scholars that a whole couplet had dropped out of the Hebrew poem. They restored it from an ancient Greek translation known as the Septuagint, which has the missing lines.

On the other hand, some bits that appear in the KJV are omitted from the RSV. For example, 1 John 5:6b–8, which was renumbered in the RSV as 7–8:

KJV	RSV
And it is the Spirit that beareth witness,	And the Spirit is the witness,

because the Spirit is truth.	because the Spirit is the truth.
For there are three that bear record in heaven,	——
the Father, the Word, and the Holy Ghost:	——
and these three are one.	——
And there are three that bear witness in earth,	There are three witnesses,
the spirit, the water, and the blood:	the Spirit, the water, and the blood;
and these three agree in one.	and these three agree.

The material omitted in the RSV is now considered by scholars to be a fourth-century addition to the Greek text, and therefore not in John's original letter.

To some, convinced in advance of the infidelity of the RSV, this change looked like a deliberate attempt to undercut the doctrine of the Trinity. It was widely publicized as "evidence" that the RSV was untrue to the Bible.

One unexpected result of the debate over the RSV was to call the attention of the church-going public (at first only in mainline churches) to the Greek and Hebrew texts.

The King James translators, three and a half centuries earlier, had used the best Greek text available to them. Since then many more manuscripts—and especially some much older ones—have been discovered. Scholars have worked over these meticulously, comparing one with another, working out the relations of one to another, and attempting to deduce the most probable form of the original from which, through various numbers of copyings, the available manuscripts had been derived. The result was that by the time of the translation of the RSV, a far better text was available than the one the KJV translators had used.

In this regard, the RSV was almost inescapably an improvement. That church people became aware of the problem was probably as significant as the fact that the RSV had a better text.

Many of the verbal changes in the RSV result from improved knowledge of the original languages. For example, at Proverbs 26:23, the KJV translates:

Burning lips and a wicked heart are like a potsherd covered with silver dross.

"Silver dross" does not make much sense in English. In fact, though the Hebrew seems to have the two words ordinarily translated "silver" and "dross," they come in the wrong order to mean this. New evidence suggests that the correct translation is "glaze." The RSV, therefore, translates:

Like the glaze covering an earthen vessel
are smooth lips with an evil heart.

This new knowledge of the original languages offers a better understanding of thousands of vocabulary items—usually only a small sharpening up of long-established meanings, but occasionally some quite drastic changes. All are important to biblical scholars; several lead to significant differences in translation.

For the general membership in the churches, the fact that the Bible could have such problems was a new idea. The general understanding was (and too often still is) that words have meanings; dictionaries tell what they are; that's it. Even a slight shift in this belief would, in the long run, have significant impact on attitudes toward the Bible.

The next critical development for the Bible came with the appearance in 1966 of *Good News for Modern Man*, a translation of the New Testament in "today's English." This translation, often called "Today's English Version," was designed primarily for use in the third world. The translators tried to find a kind of English that would be easier reading, but still thoroughly acceptable.

In planning this translation a great deal of attention was given to the kind of English used. Sample translations were tested on various sorts of English readers. It had always been assumed, generally tacitly, that close attention to vocabulary and grammar of the *source* language was necessary. It was a revolutionary idea that explicit attention also needed to be given to the *target* language. This attention to English was stimulated by the experience of missionary translators working on languages few

North Americans had ever heard of.

Much to the surprise of the American Bible Society, which had produced it, the "Good News" New Testament proved to be immensely popular with North Americans. Orders flooded in at about ten times the volume they were prepared for. Something had happened that the Bible Society had not been fully aware of.

If in the '20s and '30s most church people had learned enough "King James English" to be comfortable with it, by the '60s this had changed. Memorizing passages had decreased sharply in Sunday Schools. The close attention to specific verses—which had required comment on language differences—had gone the same way, at least in most mainline churches. The King James Version had become unintelligible to an appreciable number of church members, and to most of the general public. The Today's English Version met a real need.

The TEV's reception was best among mainline churches. Its reception was more reserved among evangelical churches; they were still gunshy after the turmoil and conflict around the RSV. Some were very negative, but others liked it. It began, slowly, to build up a following.

In the mainline churches, the TEV did not displace the RSV, but came to be used alongside it. There had long been a few who used, say, both Moffatt and the KJV, but they always kept Moffatt pretty much in the background. This was something new: two Bibles used alongside each other as equals.

Whether it was the lessons of the TEV or the spirit of the times no one can say. Evangelicals, while still holding fast to the KJV against the RSV, also began to be more open to alternative translations.

The first publication to profit from this was *The Living Bible*. It is not properly a translation, but a reworking of existing translations into a more colloquial English, achieving the same sort of sharply increased readability that had made the TEV so popular. In every other respect it is very different.

In addition to putting the text into vernacular English, the compiler inserted a great deal of explanatory material right into the text. By this it became, in a way, a much more readable sort of study Bible. Study Bibles, with copious footnotes and other helps, can quite legitimately bring in a great deal of interpretation; the user can (and should, but doesn't always) distinguish it by the fact that it is separate from the text. In *The Living Bible*, however, text and comments are indistinguishable.

Merchandised aggressively, *The Living Bible* soon became popular in many evangelical churches. It did not displace the King James, but came to be used in parallel with it. It had a function roughly like that of the TEV, in that it showed, to a constituency not reading the TEV, that intelligibility was separate from fidelity, and that there was a place for two Bibles alongside each other.

If in the '70s you had taken a census at Lighthouse, you would have found a slight majority of the Bibles in the hands of members at the services would be *The Living Bible*. Most of the rest would be King James.

There was an unjustified tendency to label the Today's English Version as "liberal." There was no question that *The Living Bible* was not "liberal." As a result, it competed successfully with the TEV among evangelicals and swept the field among fundamentalists, but got little support elsewhere.

The Living Bible could not, however, maintain its "conservative" support unchallenged. Too many liberties had been taken with the wording of the text. The inserted explanatory matter is highly partisan (even within evangelicalism). Even those who approved of its theological stand often wished to see text and comment separated.

Evangelicals increasingly felt a need for a new translation that would be soundly evangelical, that is, produced by people committed to inerrancy, and thus guaranteed to be free from any "modernist" taint whatever. It would scrupulously avoid the alleged errors in the RSV, and thus do for the conservatives what the RSV was doing for the "liberals."

A large and well-financed project recruited a strong group of biblical scholars from across the spectrum of churches considered evangelical by the organizers. All translators were explicitly committed to inerrancy, and specific guidelines were set down. The result was the publication, in 1973, of *The New International Version*.

This was supported by a merchandising campaign that exceeded anything ever done before for a Bible publication—even for *The Living Bible*. It was reinforced by a wide range of subsidiary publications which followed very quickly: concordances, study Bibles, commentaries, Greek-English and Hebrew-English parallels...

The NIV quickly became popular in the churches for which it was designed. It looked like it might, indeed, stand as the evangelical counterpart to the "liberal" RSV, and thus perpetuate the division.

Church people outside the evangelical circle were at first very suspicious of the NIV. It had, after all, been planned as a deliberate polemic tool, and it was promoted at first as partisan. When the NIV was more carefully examined, however, non-evangelicals came to recognize it as a good translation—with failings, of course, but no more faults than any other translation. It has some attractive features, among them the use of "you" where the RSV had retained "thou" in direct address to God. Increasing numbers of mainline ministers and lay people are using the NIV.

Experience with the NIV has driven home an important lesson: if the Bible text is translated with honesty by excellent scholars, party differences are minimized. We should read that two ways: The NIV, done by committed evangelicals, is a good translation because it was done honestly and carefully. Another, done by "liberals," if they are honest and competent, could also be a good translation.

The NIV has steadily, if slowly, achieved acceptance across the churches. It may, before long, cease to be in any way restricted to one party. It may, in fact, contribute to bringing about convergence in the matter of Bible translations between all factions.

Whether that convergence actually comes about or not, some convictions are spreading through both evangelical and mainline constituencies, and will almost certainly be part of any new consensus:

1. Ongoing change in the English language requires new translations from time to time.
2. Progressively improved understanding of the original languages must be reflected, from time to time, in changes in detail within our English Bible, and more importantly, in numerous minor changes of our interpretation of it.
3. No one translation can fully present our best understanding of the original text.
4. No one translation can meet the needs of all readers and all situations.
   Scholars on both sides have generally come to share a fifth conviction:
5. In some matters our understanding of the text is incomplete, and in some erroneous. For the most part these are very minor details, but the possibility is not excluded that some are of some importance.

Behind these are further elements of emerging consensus, less directly interesting to the lay membership, but fundamental in a special

way to our present concerns:
1. The authority of the Bible rests, primarily, in the Greek, Hebrew, and Aramaic originals.
2. That authority rests, practically, in the best text that careful scholarship can reconstruct.
3. Whatever authority any English translation may possess depends on its fidelity in reflecting the sense of these originals. This can never be absolute.
4. Whatever usefulness any English Bible may possess depends on a combination of qualities. One is fidelity and another intelligibility; these are of equal importance.

All in all, we are moving, across most of the church, to a more realistic understanding of what the Bible is. This is happening not only in mainline churches but equally in evangelical. Changes in the Bible North Americans know has its effect on the use of the Bible, and will on views of its authority. In the long run, this should provide the basis for a more reasoned discussion between the two divisions of the church on the authority of the Bible, and, perhaps, some convergence in the way it is used.

ACADEMIA AND THE BIBLE

Marjory Ives, a devout church-goer standing in the checkout line, can not help seeing the screaming headline, "Bible Reveals Herbal Cure for Dandruff!" That is a little discomforting; she respects the Bible and feels a vague resentment at such trivialization of it. Turning her eyes away, she notices that the man ahead is carrying a magazine. She reads the title *New Testament Studies*. She strains to make out the table of contents in small print on the cover. The only article she can see clearly is "A Diatessaric Rendering in Luke 2:7." The tabloid she understood all too well; this simply leaves her puzzled.

The professor had stopped to pick up a loaf of bread on his way home, and there he is, carrying something he wants to read that evening. In a way, he is an alien in that church-goer's world. Actually, he is only half alien; he commutes between two incongruent worlds. He stands in the checkout line and buys the loaf of bread like anyone else, but he has come, minutes ago, from academia. His life in academia revolves around the New Testament, and particularly Paul's mission to the Gentiles.

That other book he has with him, Marjory Ives does not recognize. The cover reads "H KAINH ΔIAΘHKH"; she thinks "That's all Greek to me," not realizing how right she is. It is actually the New Testament in its original language. Both of them read the Bible, but in what a different form!

The church claims the Bible as its own. So does secular society. So do several disciplines within academia. That checkout line is a micro-microcosm, a church-goer reacting to two other Bible users, with discomfort on one hand and puzzlement on the other.

On a larger scale the church's claim to the Bible, and the church's use of the Bible, must take account of both the claims of the secular world—exemplified by the tabloid press—and those of the academic world—exemplified by our professor and the publications he is carrying home with his loaf of bread.

Two days later, the Ives were invited out to dinner. There they met Harold Ashworth, professor of New Testament at Pilgrim Seminary.

Marjory immediately recognized him as that person in the checkout line ahead of her. Her curiosity on that occasion came back to mind. Rather diffidently she asked him about that magazine article and that book. Harold is fairly good at explaining things without using jargon. He had no trouble about the book. She understood immediately what the Greek New Testament was and why Harold would have it. Aware of forty years of turmoil over biblical translations, Marjory knew the Bible was not originally written in English.

The article was harder to explain. It dealt with a verse that Marjory immediately recognized:

> And she gave birth to her first-born son and wrapped him in swaddling clothes, and laid him in a manger; because there was no place for them in the inn. (Luke 2:7)

Marjory never had any particular difficulty in the passage, once "swaddling clothes" had been explained. The article dealt with a different matter. A 17th century Estonian translation has something like "no other place," instead of "no place." The extra word is claimed to reflect a very old tradition in the church going back to the Diatessaron, a weaving together of the four gospels into a single account, produced about AD 170, hence that strange word in the title.

Beyond that, Harold had difficulties explaining how so much could be argued from a single word, and why it was of interest to New Testament scholars.

There lies the crux of the matter: It is almost impossible to show outsiders what it is that Bible scholars really do and why. The problems they deal with are technical, complex, and often focus on minute details. There is a real chasm between academic Bible study and the average church's use of the Bible.

Many things in academia are baffling. For instance, many academics spend their lives experimenting with the inheritance of eye color in fruit flies. Fruit-fly genetics and Bible interpretation are about as remote as any two subjects in academia, but parallels between them illustrate how the game has changed in half a century.

Fifty years ago geneticists just crossed different strains of fruit flies, sorted those flies' offspring by eye color, and did a little simple statistical calculation. If an outsider wanted an explanation of what was going on, that was easily given.

It was harder to explain *why* anyone would want to know that much about fruit-fly eyes. But most people took that on faith; science, they thought, is both good and mysterious.

New Testament research was no more complex. A scholar got out the Greek New Testament, some dictionaries, grammars, and a concordance, and went to work, comparing one verse with another.

Today fruit-fly genetics is investigated in laboratories with hundreds of thousands of dollars worth of equipment, each piece requiring specialized personnel to operate. The computations are so extensive that they are impossible to do with paper and pencil, so you need a computer, and not just an ordinary desk-top machine.

It is a lot easier now to explain why scientists do all this: "Fruit-fly genetics is very much like human genetics. What we learn here will help us with all sorts of human genetic problems. Fruit flies are just a lot easier to work with than human beings." People are beginning to understand that science is not a mass of disconnected "facts," but a great system of interrelated concepts.

B ible problems have multiplied in complexity just about as fast. It is getting harder and harder merely to describe what is being done, just as in genetics. Unlike genetics, however, it has not gotten much easier to describe why.

At Pilgrim Seminary, Harold Ashworth works with a computer system that holds more data than a couple of shelves of books. He can get to any bit of all that almost instantly. Harold no longer has to flip pages in the concordance, and then go to another volume to hunt up the passage in the Greek Testament, and so on, back and forth between the two books. Just type a command, and the passages are all there on the screen before him. The search is much faster and easier.

But what has really happened is that he can ask much more complex questions of the text than he ever could before. Instead of the physical effort of flipping pages, he now has the mental task of formulating those more complex questions explicitly so that the computer can "understand."

The real increase in complexity, however, has come not on Ashworth's desk, but in the field of New Testament studies as a whole. The data Harold works with depend on long chains of specialists. Some comes from dusty digs in Palestine, others from equally dusty archives in Europe, and some even from investigations of the icecap in Antarctica. (Ashworth's investigations into Paul's letters need to know, for example, about global climatic shifts 20 centuries ago!)

There has also been a vast increase in the amount of data available for scholars to work with. For example, in 1947 some Bedouins chanced on a cave at Qumran near the Dead Sea and found there some ancient manuscripts. Subsequent exploration turned up many more. They turned out to be documents from a Jewish sect living in that area a little before the time of Christ. They include copies of various Old Testament books, commentaries, hymns, sectarian documents. Collectively they opened a wide window on one aspect of pre-Christian Judaism, as well as on various Old Testament textual problems, and on New Testament backgrounds.

It requires high-tech procedures just to unroll the documents, often known as the Dead Sea Scrolls, without destroying them. It takes high-tech equipment to make faded ink visible, so that other specialists can read, transcribe, and translate the texts.

Spectacular discoveries like Qumran are supplemented by many lesser finds. These range from a few fair sized documents down to many hundreds of brief memos on broken pieces of pottery. Even the shortest and most fragmentary give us data about Bible life and times.

At Pilgrim Seminary, Professor Novakova works on late Hebrew prophecy. She makes use of that Qumran material, and material from many other finds. She works with them in their published form, that is, at the end of that long series of steps, each conducted by specialists.

Professor Ashworth works on the Pauline letters. He has less direct involvement with the Qumran material. But he too must, from time to time, reckon with some little detail from Qumran.

This piling up of levels of scholarship has complicated biblical studies in recent decades. Most of the work that is being done is significant only in relation to the whole. Projects may be crucial because they tie things together deep within the overall structure of current research; such projects cannot be explained effectively to outsiders, any more than a geneticist can explain how some minor problem in fruit fly heredity fits into the broad picture.

Such research necessarily goes on in a very different atmosphere from that of a church engaged in Bible study. There is often misunderstanding on both sides.

In many churches, academics meet an undercurrent of suspicion. Few churches are comfortable with the specialized knowledge and interests of theological professors; and few theological professors are comfortable in the churches. Academic theologians can also be intimidating to the resident preacher.

A part of the disjointedness that Wesley Chalmers—and many more like him—faced in his theological education is rooted in the cultural differences between academia and the world around.

G. Whitefield Finney did not face that same disjointedness because Word Bible School had carefully shielded itself from academia. It thought that it was closing out "the world," as the New Testament enjoins. Actually, it was only shutting out one segment. By shutting out academia, though, it made itself more open to biblical secularism—or the secular Bible—than the seminaries.

As an undergraduate, I took the required "freshman English." In it we read, among other things, the Book of Esther.

For that first year English course, Esther was anthologized out of the Bible. That is to say, it was placed in a context of other readings of various kinds. This enhanced its literary significance, while diminishing its religious significance. Esther is somewhat unusual within the Bible. Among other things, it doesn't mention God. It is more than most books in the Bible open to shift by anthologization. The shift can bring its religious significance to near zero.

Of course, the Bible itself is an anthology of a different sort. Inclusion in this anthology enhances—or even creates—Esther's religious significance. The term "anthology" is not usually used in this way; "canon" is preferred. The principle, however, is the same. The canon is simply a collection of books of diverse origin brought together on the basis of their joint religious significance. Not one of the books is the same within the canon as it is or would be outside. Inclusion within the canon is crucial.

A story within the canon means more than the same story excerpted, anthologized, and de-canonized. Only in the simplest tellings, do we label the first book of the New Testament "Matthew's Story." "Gospel of Matthew" says something important about the nature of that canonical document and its message.

On the surface, the tabloid's headline about the Bible had nothing in common with an English department's use. The tabloid's treatment was crude, sensational, irreverent, frequently trivial, and often verging on the fraudulent. The literary approach is refined, scholarly, respectful, significant, and honest. Yet they have something in common. Both have decanonized those portions—large or small—that they wish to deal with. What they produce depends, crucially, on the new context they put it into. The tabloid wants to sell papers; the English department wants to develop literary appreciation.

The church can learn from that: the context in which the Bible is read is of fundamental importance. Instinctively, it has acted on that basis. The primary context in which the Bible is read in the churches is worship—most likely the same context in which the canon was formed. That is the context in which its true value can best be grasped.

When scraps of the Bible are placed in a context of scandal, sensationalism, and hype, they are de-canonized. When prooftexts are torn from the Bible and hurled at opponents in argument, the same thing happens.

For the church, the Bible is more than English literature. It cuts across all languages. It is the Bible as surely in Hottentot as in English, and as certainly in English as in Greek. The Greek is only first among equals. All languages are joined in the Bible. All versions share in holding Christians together.

English literature is shot through with allusions. For much of it, no understanding is possible without a good foundation in the Bible (and the classics).

More than any other source—even Shakespeare—the King James Bible has supplied allusions in English literature. Therefore, every serious student of English literature should know the Bible, and preferably the King James. That is why English departments have fought against some of the new translations. They wish to preserve the old wording, and not only the old wording—the old interpretation, the interpretation on which English authors have traditionally based their allusions.

This scholarly concern is legitimate. Perhaps we have abandoned too unfeelingly the version to which we owe so much. So also is the church's claim that the clear and cogent presentation of the message must not be subordinated to nostalgia or literary tradition. These two concerns must be reconciled.

The basis is at hand: we have learned that two translations, say the TEV and the RSV, can work together in making the message come alive, each supplementing the other. We are coming to a fundamental commitment to pluralism in versions within the churches' use. Can that not be enlarged to accommodate two different uses of the Bible? Two different sorts of Bible knowledge and of Bible scholarship?

We in the church might well ask more seriously what we can learn from the literary scholars as they continue their work with the King James, and we might encourage and support them in it. We might request them to look also at some of the new versions—say the *New Revised Standard Version*—from their special vantage point. Perhaps they have more to offer to the church than we realize.

Seminary teaching of the Bible is in some ways the exact opposite of that in the English department. The emphasis is on the religious message. The passages examined are put into a context that brings the meaning out as clearly as possible. The studies are always kept in the context of the canon, the whole set of biblical books. They are also kept in the context of the apostolic community (for the New Testament), and of the religious experience of Israel (for the Old Testament). Those contexts are clarified through additional information about the Near Eastern environment, Canaanite religion, the early church, first century Judaism, the Hellenistic civilization...

The literary qualities of the passages are not suppressed, merely subordinated. The message—the religious message, that is—is reinforced by the literary form.

Moreover, the concern tends to be more with the literary form of the original than of the translation. Introductory Old Testament courses devote a brief discussion to Hebrew poetry and its base in specific features of the language and in specific sorts of language use.

All this contributes to the confusion among church members about what the Bible is, and means.

It's reasonable for people like Marjory Ives to assume that there is just one Bible. Only when Marjory—and others like her—recognize that there are several Bibles, which may use the same books and chapters and verses, does some of the confusion unravel itself.

One of those Bibles is the secular Bible, appropriated by the tabloids and the English departments as a cultural artifact.

Another is the academic Bible, dissected and examined for subtle nuances of meaning. The details of this study may seem too minute to matter, let alone to understand; collectively, they enhance the meaning and significance of the third Bible, the religious canon.

The Bible studied in churches and in seminary is the canon, somehow by the grace of God pulled together into a single more-or-less unified text. Ultimately, that is what gives the Bible a prominent place in every curriculum. That is what makes all the tension worthwhile. The academic view helps to understand the Bible as canon; being canon gives the Bible a place in the life of the church.

The Willing Workers' Class at Nazareth United Church accepted the Bible rather naively as the "Word of God." Rufus Bartram could meet them on that basis because, though he understood a much more complex process in the formation of the Bible, he too saw it as the canon, as speaking the Word. So, as Mrs. Dougal McAllister said, "Every Sunday he gives us something interesting and inspiring, and right down the line with the Bible."

THE SECULAR BIBLE

Millions standing in checkout lines saw the headline "Bible Reveals Herbal Cure for Dandruff." Many felt discomfort, as Marjory Ives did. Many others were amused. Some had their interest aroused or hope kindled. The issue sold out. That headline did its part to attract buyers. It can, therefore, tell us something about North Americans.

That article was an example of one common tabloid theme: the announcement of a startling new remedy for some human affliction. The favorite problem is overweight; wrinkles and hair-loss follow close behind. Every such headline invokes some authority. It may be a "personality" (always mentioned by name), scientists or doctors (as a class, never specifically identified), or the Bible. Readers trust any of these.

There is a vaguely religious aspect in many of the headlines. Every month or so a tabloid proclaims new "proof" of life after death (or transmigration of souls—the tabloids seem unclear on the difference). One was a child that talked at birth, another a departed spouse who stopped in for dinner. These events answer religious yearnings. Some people take them to verify "biblical" convictions—that's why they are often hawked as "new evidence."

In many other matters, the Bible is cited directly. Predictions for the next year are popular, and generally mix the musings of psychics with a little pseudo-biblical prophecy. Finding UFOs described in the Bible is good for an article every year or so. A recent article reported how a millionaire misplaced his Bible and lost his fortune, only to regain it when the Bible was found.

Solutions to biblical puzzles have a special appeal. Was it really an apple that tempted Adam and Eve? Science now has the answer! The "ten lost tribes of Israel" keep turning up in odd corners of the world. Noah's ark must still rest where it landed; every few years it is found again. A handful of such Bible stories have a special hold on the North American imagination.

For a recent Christmas, a two-year-old acquaintance received a plastic boat containing eight pairs of brightly colored plastic animals. His Bible education had begun, as it had for thousands of other children who received that same toy.

What the child learns from the toy will be reinforced through picture books, and then story books. Noah will take his place alongside Santa Claus and Bugs Bunny—all parts of the child's world. 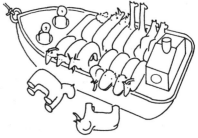 Though such a North American child will learn about Noah, some things can very easily be missed: Noah's faithfulness among a dissolute people, or God's covenant with Noah. The story, as it is most widely known, is about Noah's floating zoo, not about God's dealing with Noah or Noah's response.

Noah is probably the Bible story most children first encounter, but it is by no means the last. Joseph and his coat, Jonah and the whale, David and Goliath are all memorable stories. All will be heard outside the biblical canon. They will be mixed with stories of Washington and the silver dollar or Laura Secord and her cows, Goldilocks, the hare and the tortoise, the Grinch, and Ninja Turtles—or whatever succeeds them as a popular fad.

As the child gets older, all this is sorted out more or less, always in the categories of the secular culture.

At some point, the child will find out "the truth about Santa Claus and the Easter Bunny." He or she will learn the grown-up's responsibility toward these stories: don't believe them, but in the presence of young children, act as if you do.

The maturing child will learn that one sort of story always begins "Once upon a time..." These all fit into a class called "fairy tales." No one seriously asks whether they are true, any more than they ask whether they are polyunsaturated.

A class of fables will emerge, and the child will learn about the fox and the grapes, the hare and the tortoise, the old man and his donkey, and several others as examples of fables.

The child will learn that some familiar stories come from the Bible. Like legends, fairy tales and fables, Bible stories are told in their own way, and have their own functions. These stories one does not disbelieve, at least not openly. Indeed, some adults firmly believe they are true. In this respect Bible stories are different from the Santa Claus legends or fairy tales.

In western culture, however, either firm belief or sharp rejection is suspect. The safe tactic is to believe them *just a little.*

Something important is lacking in these Bible stories. David and Goliath becomes little more than a battle between the little guy and the big guy. We always like to see the little guy win, especially if he or she can win by using low-tech means. The story of Jacob isn't particularly meaningful until it is seen in relationship to Abraham and Isaac on one side and Moses and the Exodus on the other—that is, as an episode in an ongoing story of God's dealing with Israel. When it is divorced from the canon, that side of the story gets lost.

Taken out of the canon, not one of these is in any full sense the biblical story. Try the test in Second Timothy 3:16: "All Scripture is...profitable for teaching, for reproof, for correction, and for training in righteousness." The typical popularized Bible story qualifies only very weakly, if at all; it is more profitable for entertainment, with perhaps just a touch of moralizing. It is a bit of the secularized Bible that is so prominent on this continent—not of the genuine Bible.

Another child is raised in a church family and begins Sunday School very early. There she learns more Bible stories. As she progresses through the grades, she learns more and more of the religious significance of the stories. She begins to build a very different understanding of the Bible.

She has a problem, however. She continues to hear and absorb much of the popular Bible lore around her. Two different views of the Bible—almost two different Bibles—compete within her.

We sometimes think of Christian education at the elementary level as introducing the Bible. But it can't be that; the toy makers, the children's book publishers, and scores of other agencies in our culture beat the Sunday School to it. Rather, the task of the Christian education program is to *desecularize* the Bible.

Actually, the traditional Sunday School has two opposing effects. It feeds the popular biblicism of context-free tales and superficial moralizing. At the same time it struggles to put deeper meaning into the biblical passages. The concern, today, over the Sunday School might better be addressed to this fact. What is the balance of its secularizing and desecularizing? Is it an efficient instrument for pulling children away from the secular Bible? Does it hold up the faith of the Bible, or just the catchy narratives?

In my later childhood, I would occasionally hear slightly off-color stories about Santa Claus. These stories were a device to show that you didn't believe in Santa Claus, that you were "grown up." They were also a mild form of rebellion.

A little later, humorous versions of Bible stories became another vehicle for rebellion. The following verses, from a never-ending series, represent one of the popular songs:

> Adam was a gardener and Eve she was his spouse,
> They got the sack for stealing fruit and took to keeping house.
> Everything was quiet and peaceful in the main,
> 'Til they had a baby boy and took to raising Cain.
>
> Esau was a cowboy of the wild and wooly make;
> Half the farm belonged to him and half belonged to Jake.
> Now Esau thought his title to the farm was none too clear,
> So he sold it out to Jakey for a sandwich and a beer.

Some of the inaccuracies are deliberate for comic effect. Some missing details are inevitable when a story has to be told in four lines. But some distortion in the tales reflects and reinforces a general fuzziness in the tradition. As parts of the popular lore, they are fair game for improvisation and creative retelling.

Such songs usually have an incidental barb or two against some segment of the church.

The general public's attitudes toward religious institutions are deeply ambivalent. Nothing illustrates this better than the Salvation Army. There is a widespread respect for the Army and its social work that takes concrete form in fairly generous support from members of other churches and from the unchurched. On the other hand, the Army is the butt of jokes, some aimed at religion generally. Street preaching, more common a few years ago than now, was a good target:

> A Salvation Army officer was preaching on a street corner. A heckler asked her:
> "Do you really believe that the whale swallowed Jonah?"

"Yes sir, I do!"

"How can you be sure?"

"It says so right here in my Bible."

"How can you know the Bible has it right?"

She thought a bit and then said:

"Well, when I get to heaven, I'll look up Jonah and ask him."

"Suppose he isn't there?"

"Then you ask him!"

It is uncertain whether this anecdote reflects the popular feeling about Bible stories, or the popular assessments of the Salvation Army's understanding of Bible stories. For many it was probably both. Many North Americans laugh at those who staunchly believe the story of Jonah, but they half believe it themselves.

It is clear, however, that stories like this one indicate a popular attitude deprecating or ridiculing organized religion, while retaining some crumbs of religious convictions. This is another fragment of the heritage of classical evangelicalism. It was a lay movement, operating largely outside the churches or uneasily within them. It fostered a lay distrust of the organized church at the same time it built a society-wide allegiance to the Bible. The fringes of evangelicalism trivialized their Bible and reinforced their distrust.

Moreover, the story implies that anyone who does not believe the story of Jonah and the whale is destined for hell. No question is raised about anything beyond simple belief in this single episode—neither what Jonah was running away from, nor what Jonah ultimately learned. It is the superficialities of the story, taken out of context, that one is expected to believe. The story is put on a par with Noah's marine menagerie, as far as being in any real sense biblical.

The story about the Salvation Army preacher says as much about the place of heaven and hell in popular lore as it does about Jonah. Some rather odd ideas are standard.

A popular single-frame cartoon series running in a major newspaper has a number of standard settings: a corporate board room, a jail cell or park bench with two former businessmen. Frequently two men stand naked in flames belt-high, exchanging some remarks about their former business activities. On jagged rocks, rising above the fires, stand guards with tails and horns, bearing tridents.

Common are cartoons showing people in long white robes, with little wings sprouting from their shoulders, halos above their heads, and bearing a "harp" of a sort that looks about as functional as the wings. They stand on individual clouds. Why they aren't bored to death I can't imagine!

Another competing image of heaven is almost as common: St. Peter stands at the pearly gates, like an immigration officer at the Ambassador Bridge, checking applicants for admission. A variety of ideas surround this figure, some just slightly believed, and some widely accepted, as long as they don't rock the boat.

These popular pictures of heaven and hell can be traced back to medieval interpretations of the Bible. The images of hell have been elaborated by revival preaching, which often aimed to scare people into heaven with lurid depictions of the sinner's fate. The images of heaven have been trivialized by sentimentalism and moralism, and especially by equating the joys of heaven with the pleasures of this world. Where preachers and Sunday School teachers have left off, cartoonists and secular humorists have taken over.

The resulting stereotypes have moved farther and farther from the Bible. Yet they are often assumed to be biblical. Heaven and hell are sometimes taken more seriously than they deserve, and sometimes much less. The ambivalence produces a certain lightheartedness about heaven and hell in popular usage.

If even a well-informed Christian tries to read seriously any Bible passage dealing with judgment, these images of heaven and hell are hard to escape completely. They lurk in the back of the mind, warping interpretation. They dull the sharp edge of the Bible. The evangelical Bible reader is probably more seriously affected at this point. In other places, the secular view of the Bible misleads the "liberal" more heavily. For each, excluding extraneous notions derived from the secularized Bible is a major problem. It often goes unrecognized. Harps, wings and halos can all be fitted into any single mention of heaven, as can devils with tails, horns, and tridents into any mention of hell read by itself. These extra-biblical details fade, however, as the Bible is read more comprehensively.

The secularized Bible is fragmented. The surviving fragments are haphazardly selected. Out of context they are prey to twisting and misshaping. To correct this distortion, the Bible must be seen as a whole, as a canon.

The lore about the Bible itself is just as diverse, fragmented, and contradictory as that derived from its content.

During the Second World War, pocket testaments with steel covers were popular. There were stories of servicemen carrying one in their shirt pocket over their heart, where it saved their life in battle. Even if it did not deflect a bullet, a New Testament was seen as some sort of protection.

There used to be a lot of people, and there still are some, who feel the same way about having a Bible in the house, especially a family Bible on the table in the sitting room.

North American courts often require witnesses to take an oath on the Bible. It does not matter whether he or she is an earnest Christian, an unchurched person, or even a Christian at all—every witness automatically goes through that same ritual. Strangely, that oath on the Bible seems, for all alike, to have about the same effect. People are a little more honest than they might otherwise be. There is some special power ascribed to that black leather-covered book.

The secular view of the Bible has its most damaging affect in a myth. The myth seems innocent enough, even attractive. Both "liberals" and evangelicals easily accept it in some form or other. That myth is this: The Bible is a good moral book. In fact, it is *the* good moral book.

This means, first, that the Bible is uplifting to read. Actually, few in the general public are eager enough to be uplifted to read it. But it used to be prescribed in school for just this reason. We are always more interested in the uplifting of others in our charge than of ourselves. To maintain this view, we hide from ourselves some of the less attractive stories. We make it seem, for example, that God loved David because he led an exemplary life. (He didn't—as the Bible itself makes very clear, several times.) It follows that God will love us too, if we lead exemplary lives.

Second, the Bible is seen as an important support for all our democratic institutions. That was clear enough in old Springfield where the clergy were active in every public event. Nowadays we are a little less ostentatious about it. Yet we church people lead ourselves to believe that God loves our social and political system because it, like David, is exemplary.

Third, Scripture supports all public virtues. Both Canada and the United States are "Christian countries." Public virtues are generated, defined, and sustained by the Bible. Scripture also condemns all crimes and is the foundation of our criminal law. That function, somehow, centers in the Ten Commandments.

For example, the Ten Commandments are considered to condemn murder, which is obviously a seriously anti-social behavior. "Murder" is defined as killing other human beings—except: 1) in self-defense, 2) in defense of innocent women and children, 3) perhaps, even, in defense of basic property rights, 4) when merely due to carelessness, 5) when done by the state as punishment, 6) when done by the military...

Moreover, it makes a great deal of difference who the victim is. Murder of important public figures is so serious, it has a special term "assassination"—much worse than simple, everyday "murder." Next come police officers. Then ordinary citizens in good standing. Then bums sleeping on park benches, and street girls. By the time you get to peasants overseas, it is a bit questionable whether "murder" is the right word. If those peasants have communist leanings—or merely if their leaders do—it may be not "murder" but some political virtue.

All that—the general principle and its exceptions and elaborations—is allegedly established by four words: "Thou shalt not kill." Certainly something else must be involved to establish so much.

It might be further verses in the Bible, clarifying, qualifying, and sharpening this brief command. If so, the average "solid citizen" has no idea where they might be; nor does he or she have the patience to go searching for them.

Actually, it doesn't pay to look too hard. The most direct and explicit interpretation of the commandment is found in Matthew 5:21–22:

> "You have heard that it was said to the men of old, 'You shall not kill; and whoever kills shall be liable to judgment.' But I say to you that everyone who is angry with his brother shall be liable to judgment..."

That application of the commandment leads in precisely the opposite direction, making it more absolute rather than providing various qualifications and loopholes. When we consider the crime of murder, the Sermon on the Mount has to be shunted aside.

If that is not the basis, the best explanation is equally simple. Obviously the Bible, as a good moral book, must support what everybody knows to be good moral principles, especially those that are also practical. Therefore, since killing police officers is obviously worse than killing drug pushers, that must be what is meant. And so on. The Ten Commandments must be interpreted in the light of our modern needs, and the "realities" of life, as our culture understands them.

The Bible is thoroughly secularized by being subordinated to the demands of the culture, and by being forced to support the culture. Our culture has taken possession of the Bible, and will not easily tolerate any challenge to its use.

Nor will our culture tolerate any indiscriminate use of the Bible, particularly "anti-social" use. It is acceptable to quote the Bible against murder; the Bible obviously has it right there. Or against any other crimes or breaches of good social order. But there are limits.

Leviticus 19:9–10 is an example of a passage requiring great care. It reads as follows:

> "When you reap the harvest of your land, you shall not reap your field to its very border, neither shall you gather the gleanings after the harvest. And you shall not strip your vineyard bare, neither shall you gather the fallen grapes of your vineyard; you shall leave them for the poor and the sojourner. I am the Lord your God."

It is only a slight generalization to see this as requiring people with income to provide support for the poor, and even the penniless foreign immigrant ("the sojourner"). The passage is, moreover, in close context with "you shall love your neighbor as yourself"—the second great commandment, identified by Jesus.

There are several possible responses to the suggestion that this commandment applies in our society today:

- "The Bible really couldn't say that, could it? That would take away all incentive to work. Why, our whole economic system could fall apart. Besides, the Bible does have a message for the lazy: 'Go to the ant, O sluggard.' (Proverbs 6:6)"
- "That's just for farmers."
- "I don't understand that old-fashioned Bible English very well; it probably doesn't mean what you say it does. The Bible doesn't have that kind of nonsense in it."
- "It couldn't really say that, could it? Maybe it's a bad translation."
- "You must be quoting out of context."

Or simply...

- "I don't believe you."

But the more polite and reasoned response is

- "That's an economic question, not a moral or theological matter. Economics and morality are quite separate. Economics is one area where you have to be absolutely realistic. It's a hard-nosed matter. So we had better keep the Bible out of it."

The secularized Bible knows to whom it belongs, and what its master requires of it. It never intrudes in economic matters.

Nobody in old Springfield ever asked the question, of course. But almost everyone would know the answer, if it had been asked: the Bible was against Irish whiskey, but not against barrels.

THE BIBLE
IN CONFLICT

The denomination to which I belong, The United Church of Canada, was created in 1925 by merging Methodist, Presbyterian, and Congregational traditions. It was the first major church union across denominational families; there have since been a number of others in various parts of the world. The United Church of Canada has been proud of that leadership, and it has always found a special satisfaction in its diversity. That it has in ample measure.

"United Church" sometimes seems like a case of mislabeling. The name implies some unity in practice and, especially, in thought. Sometimes, however, the multilingual, multicultural hubbub pretty well conceals the common creed.

Some congregations use the lectionary; others will have nothing to do with it. In some the preacher wears alb and stole; in others the old Geneva gown and bands; in still others no special attire of any kind is tolerated. Some congregations are bastions of social and political conservatism; some others seem to be composed of a seething mass of social activists; most somehow hold the whole range together in one worshipping community.

The United Church of Canada has thought of itself, also, in some peculiar way, as a national church with a special mandate to serve as the social conscience of Canada. There is some tension over how this is supposed to work. Some restrict the social-conscience function to the traditional areas: temperance, public decency and, particularly today, opposition to gambling. Others would like to keep The United Church at the front, pioneering new issues, breaking ground for the other churches, who will follow in a decade or two. Generally, the two outlooks prod the church to simultaneous action in both areas. Thus it may be defending "a common day of rest" (formally "Sabbath observance") on the one hand, and opposing missile testing in Canada's north on the other.

Occasionally there are internal clashes. Abortion is a case in point. The church includes ardent pro-life members, equally ardent pro-choice members, a large group that would gladly take a stand if only they could see one side as clearly better, and another large group that simply wishes that the issue would go away so the church could concentrate on something less controversial.

The United Church is a nation-wide network of congregations, presbyteries, and conferences, all bristling with committees, subcommittees, task forces, and all the rest. It acts like a gigantic net stretched from sea to sea that catches any issue that swims by—or that just drifts in. Moreover, some members of the church seem to make a career of converting events into issues. Everyone in Canada with some special cause that can be made to look even vaguely progressive sees The United Church as a potential ally. Thus The United Church is perpetually awash in social issues.

That mass of issues is not homogeneous. Some are local and some are regional, national, or international. Some are perennial; some are sudden crises. Some are of ultimate importance; some turn out to have been trivial. Some are resolved satisfactorily; some get nowhere.

When there is a debate, the arguments can be based on science, social science, literature, folk lore, prejudice, stereotypes, free imagining, or whatever. They are pretty much the same arguments as might be used outside the church—with one exception.

T he one exception is that, when things get contentious, the Bible is brought in. There is a general feeling in the church that the Bible ought to settle things. After all, the Bible is our common standard; we all agree on that.

The sad fact is that the Bible seldom settles anything. Both sides quote from it. We end up with new eddies in the controversy. They swirl around the relevance of a passage to the issue at hand, or around the proper interpretation. One party claims to be biblical, implying that their opponents are not. In return, the first party is charged with being "literalists," or "prooftexters," or whatever pejorative equivalent comes to hand. A battle about almost any issue at all can be quickly transmuted into a battle about who is true to the biblical heritage of the denomination, or simply true to the Bible.

There has been a growing feeling in the church that the answer must be a better understanding of the place of the Bible. So we have reacted in the characteristic United Church way. We have set up committees, commissions, working groups, task forces and study groups all across the church to look into the matter. If we can get one of these working in every congregation, every presbytery, every conference, and at the national level, then, obviously, the matter will be solved. (Anyone who says that "The United Church of Canada doesn't believe in anything" simply hasn't understood the church. It surely believes in committees!)

Questions crop up. Why doesn't the Bible settle the issues? What can be done to improve the situation?

The simplistic answer to that first question is that there are conflicting notions on the authority of the Bible. That is thought to explain why two parties can interpret the same Bible and get diametrically opposed answers.

Superficially, that answer makes sense. The press carries reports on the evangelical churches. They take a definite, unequivocal stand, claimed to be Bible-based. They are known as having a straightforward, simple, agreed-upon understanding on the "authority of the Bible": inerrancy. Armed with that, it seems, they can go to the Bible and get a definitive, black-and-white answer. What The United Church needs, it is argued, is a similarly straightforward, definitive, simple, agreed-upon doctrine of the authority of Scripture.

That, however, is at least partially an illusion. Inerrantists do not always come up with the same answers; they can come up with radically conflicting positions. When they do agree, it is because they share much more than a common position on the Bible. Remember that a great deal of the preaching at Lighthouse is devoted to building up a consistent, shared body of doctrine. In most similar churches, quite closely similar doctrinal systems have been taught. It is that tradition of interpretation which actually gives the definitive answers, not the Bible itself.

Lack of a single tradition of interpretation is not an adequate explanation for the failure of the Bible to resolve the contentious issues in The United Church. Something else contributes.

My first guess is this: controversy is not a context in which to do good Bible interpretation. No common doctrine about the Bible or tradition can assure common answers in such an atmosphere. Under the best of conditions, an interpreter must guard against reading his or her preconceived solution into the Bible. The more there seems to be at stake, the more difficult this is. Moreover, the Holy Spirit is not easily heard over anger.

The problem lies in part with the nature of the Bible, in part with what we expect of it. Our expectations simply do not fit comfortably with its character. The church's side of the problem is inherited. Luther and Calvin urged a return to the Bible. On one hand, they went to the Bible to reform worship and piety. On the other, they used the Bible first to oppose Rome, then to battle each other. Their successors sharpened the biblical weapons further. The reformation legacy of the Bible as a weapon continues to haunt us today.

But if polemic is not a proper use for the Bible, neither must we set Scripture aside whenever we find ourselves in conflict. The Bible has a function in reconciliation. It also has a function in guiding reconciled Christians as they seek, in fellowship, to be faithful. Controversy within the church is, therefore, a clear call to bring in the Bible.

Bible study can reconcile disputants, but only when they are willing to set aside their preconceptions and prejudices, when they are willing to sit down and read together, to seek an interpretation that they can share, and to open themselves to the leading of the Holy Spirit. The same kind of Bible reading can avert hostilities and make debate constructive.

So one question must be eliminated: "How should we use the Bible in debate?" Two others must take its place: "How can we use the Bible in reconciliation?" and "How can we use the Bible for guidance in faithfulness?"

Not every issue is so contentious that party lines harden and the Bible becomes a battle weapon. What of the instance where the church, or some part of it goes to the Bible seeking the will of God in some particular matter? In this situation, appeal to the Bible is entirely legitimate. There are, however, always two quite different questions: hermeneutics and authority.

"Hermeneutics" is one of those jargon words that contributes to the misunderstanding between theologians and Bible-readers-in-the-pews. For professionals, it labels *the whole discipline of Bible interpretation, the principles of finding out what the Bible says*. It examines the various steps in the process, and the various alternatives at each step. It tries to ask all the hard questions about method and validity. Hermeneutics asks these questions in general, not merely in specific cases.

I could avoid the term, of course, but in a discussion like this even this jargon term can have a function: "Hermeneutics" emphasizes that determining what the Bible says is never a simple matter. A complex mass of problems interrelate, and must be considered together. "Hermeneutics" also helps to make clear that these issues must be addressed in general, not merely in specific cases as they come up in reading the Bible.

On the down side, hermeneutic discussion can raise so many picky little problems that no one ever gets to actually reading. Professionals always make simple matters complex, if they can. In the long run, though, the risk is worth it. The occasional diversion from the real question is minor compared with the traps that can be avoided.

The distinction, then, is between two questions:

• Hermenuetics—How do we find out what the Bible says?
• Authority—What hold does that have on us?

The first question is largely technical, the second theological.

Hermeneutics is a major concern in theological seminaries. It is always in the background of any work with the Bible. Scholarly work is meticulous about hermeneutical principles. When academics tear each other's work apart (it's euphemistically called "peer review") any unsound or debatable hermeneutic practice is laid bare.

In many years of active participation in the "courts of the church" (the bodies that make decisions for the denomination and its parts), I have heard little reference to hermeneutics, whether labeled as such or not. There, people argue about the interpretation of a specific passage, but not about the principles involved.

On the other hand, I have heard much more discussion of authority in the courts of the church than at theological seminaries. Authority seems to be the particular principle that attracts the attention of the general membership.

So when conflict arises, we wring our hands over a lack of consensus on the "authority of the Bible." More often it is a difference in hermeneutics. If that is the case, no refinement of our statements on authority will have much effect. Statements may well be useful for some other reason, but they will not cure our bickering.

One pervading problem is distinguishing what the text actually says from what it is generally believed to say. We saw in old Springfield a simple illustration. The door of the high school carried that inscription:

"Ye shall know the truth, and the truth shall make you free." In the educational context, the meaning seems evident: truth is what is taught in schools. The biblical meaning is something quite different: truth is what we see in Christ.

The last chapter pointed out some of the more blatant examples of taking the biblical passages out of context. In the secularized Bible, themes are distorted, elaborated on, and trivialized. Particularly in matters of public policy we—all of us, not just one party—are open to being influenced by this store of public "Bible" lore.

What we do not distort, we often merely skip over. We all know the story of the tower of Babel, or of Noah, but do we remember the message?

The only way to avoid either error is to read more widely, more attentively, and with greater understanding of the biblical world. In particular, it is to read the individual passages within the canon.To read them in isolation from the canon of Scripture is inevitably to misread them.

Bible translation has produced what is almost a new Bible. The changes may seem superficial and minor, but their consequences are not. The book now must be read in a different way from the Bible of a century ago. I suggest that it must be read with the experts.

With, not *by*. There are denominations where staff (bishops, teachers, editors…) lay down the official interpretation. Ordinary members are encouraged to read, but are directed what to find in the text. Perhaps the Jehovah's Witnesses provide the most familiar example in our day. That Witness who rings your doorbell, to explain some passage of Scripture, gives you exactly the same interpretation as every other Witness; it is what they were all taught to say.

There are also local churches where the pastor does all the interpreting. Sometimes the pastor is dominant and quite assured of his or her own superior ability. More often the lay members suffer from a broad streak of laziness. Why should we struggle with the text when the Rev can do it for us—and so much better?

There are also places where the Sunday School does the interpreting *for* the people (or for the children). That was more common a generation or so back. Reginald Scott worked hard at making his teachers' meetings useful. He always came up with some good stuff for his staff, and they obediently passed it along to the pupils. Unfortunately, he did this apart from the pastor and the rest of the congregation. One result was disjointedness. Another was a disproportionate emphasis on Bible stories as stories, feeding popular biblical lore. None of those patterns of interpretation by "experts" are approved in mainline Protestant churches. (Nor for that matter in good evangelical churches!) All believe in the ministry of the whole people of God under the Scriptures, and therefore in the obligation of all members to read the Bible. But in our culture, where responsibility is so easily delegated, we quickly fall into leaving biblical interpretation to the paid specialist.

Scripture must be read *with* the experts. That does not mean, merely, that lay members should read with the clergy, though in most places that is, obviously, the first step. Rather, all reading should be connected to the whole body of scholarship. The minister, most likely with an M.Div. from a seminary, may provide an important link in that. But he or she is only a link, and not the only link either.

No church is fulfilling its responsibilities that does not provide a library of reference works for its members. (In my own denomination, most congregations provide a book allowance for the pastor. It is much larger than the allowance for the church library—if there is one.) Nor is the church fulfilling its responsibilities if it leaves its members ignorant of the use of these references.

In a wider context, seminaries are another link. Professors Ashworth and Novakova were both dependent on, and tied in with, a great network of scholarship for their research. In this way, these two professors are links also—Professor Novakova especially, with European scholarship not easily accessible to many of her colleagues. Unfortunately, their connections to scholarship are stronger than their connections to the churches.

Academic institutions are a crucial resource for the church. For most mainline denominations, though, church-related colleges teaching liberal arts have slipped away. They are now often totally secular in their educational emphasis. But the seminaries we still have—though they tend to have a closer association with the university than with the church. We usually think of seminaries solely as trainers of church professionals. But they should be much more; they could be links between the churches and scholarship.

Evangelicalism in North America has traditionally set a wall with a narrow, guarded gate between itself and academic scholarship. The Bible School that Whitefield Finney attended exemplifies one extreme. It was closely in touch with the churches that supported it, but heavily insulated from academia.

Another pattern has been the evangelical seminary, perhaps a little less closely in touch with its churches, and a little more open to academia. Its professors were trained at prestigious universities and seminaries, but carefully selected to ensure that they were not infected with "modernism." One of their tasks was to sort through academic publications to select those items that would support their seminary's doctrinal stand, and to reject anything questionable. The seminary was a filter, passing on to the churches only what the churches wanted.

But evangelical seminaries are changing. They accept more from scholarship, and contribute more to it. As Wesley Chalmers noticed, many more evangelical publications are useful to him today than they were fifteen years ago.

The mainline seminaries have tried to maintain open interchange with every relevant segment of academia. They demand much less doctrinal conformity from their faculty. But they do, generally, insist on academic qualifications and research under prevailing academic standards. Occasionally that policy results in publication of a book or article that seems highly suspicious to church leaders—if they happen to see it.

In principle there is an open interchange with the churches. In fact, there is relatively little traffic. The churches, even those rooted in the "liberal" side of old controversies, retain at least a touch of suspicion of the seminaries and of academic scholarship. The seminary faculty members are uncomfortable in the churches, inexpert at speaking at a non-academic level, or just too busy to do very much. Lay people seldom go near the seminaries, and many of the clergy are too far away to make much use of their facilities.

Evangelical professors have, by and large, done a much better job of communicating with the laity—a glance over the shelves in any "Christian book store" will demonstrate that. But, of course, they have an easier task. They are not so often called on to explain the relevance of new discoveries from Qumran, or the latest trend in hermeneutics.

The gap between seminary professor and Bible-reader-in-the-pew is wide. But it is not unbridgeable. Rufus Bartram in the Willing Workers Class at Nazareth Corners bridged it. Howard Ashworth chatting at dinner with Marjory Ives bridged it too. Zdenka Novakova is a link too, especially for some of the churches of recent immigrants, whose life and problems she understands better than most of her colleagues. The challenge today is to find ways to bring thousands of churches, and hundreds of thousands of church members, into such bridges.

It requires a new faith among the people. Biblical scholarship is threatening to leaders like Reginald Scott, the Sunday School superintendent, and to many whose Bible education has been similarly limited. They find discussion of hermeneutical problems discomforting. The Bible is not a simple book. Any simple view of it will find exposure to modern biblical scholarship an initial shock. But that shock can be overcome. What is needed is a broader view of inspiration and of canon. If the Gospels were written on the basis of strands of oral tradition, that does not detract from its message; the apostolic church which transmitted that material was under the Lordship of Christ and the inspiration of the Holy Spirit. If the early church debated long and hard over the Epistle to the Hebrews before it was finally included, inspiration must have guided the decision. God can speak just as well through a complexly-formed Pentateuch as through one written exclusively by Moses.

No one, really, has anything to fear if Matthew's account differs from Luke's, or if James sometimes seems opposed to Paul. The question is not which one is right, nor how one can be harmonized with the other—both very human questions—but what each contributes to the fullness of the Gospel message.

Not everything proposed by academics is valuable, of course. But everything is worth critical examination. The church must step cautiously around the academic appetite for novelty, and winnow out what is helpful. The church must select, not on the basis of what fits preconceived doctrine, but rather on the basis of what sheds light on the Scriptures in all their complexity.

Academic Bible study can deepen faith, and in the long run is sure to. *If we cannot hold to that assurance, we have no faith in the Bible.*

All church people stand, in a deepened sense, with the president of Whitefield Finney's Bible School when he told the graduates, "the Bible is a wondrous book, full of truth to extend through a lifetime of Bible study and more." He spoke not of our lifetime only, but the lifetime of the whole church.

TWO VIEWS ON AUTHORITY

The real issue is Bible *use and authority*, not simply authority of Scripture. This is the thesis put forward in my first chapter. In looking at Lighthouse Bible Church and Central United Church I have marshalled a mass of evidence in support of this thesis.

My discussions with Wesley Chalmers suggest that he will go along, that, when he reads this book, he will agree that I have sustained the argument. I am equally sure that G. Whitefield Finney's reaction will be the opposite. He will continue to insist that authority is the real issue. He will admit that there are differences in the use of the Bible, but either they are direct consequences of accepting or rejecting inerrancy or they are relatively trivial matters.

Yet the debate today, both in the United churches and in many sister churches, centers on the "authority of the Bible." That is to say, it starts more nearly from Finney's understanding of the *question* than from Chalmers'—or mine. It does not proceed as Finney would conduct it, so there is contradiction built in. It may not come in the end to Finney's *answer* or to anything close to it, and so the answer never quite fits the question. Perhaps that is why so many in the United churches seem a little uncomfortable with the debate.

Nevertheless, the debate continues. However much I might wish it might be broadened or redirected, it will continue to focus all too narrowly on "authority." We cannot dismiss the question because we do not like the way it is set. Nor can we establish a new starting point. Somehow we must first face the question of "authority" and then go on to the broader more meaningful question.

That suggests that we should look again at Chalmers and Finney, focusing more sharply on their ideas of authority. We want to see more precisely just how they, and others standing with them, differ on this part of the larger issue.

Wesley Chalmers is aware that others—old and young, men and women—use the Bible much as he does and hold the same view of it. They are not just in his own United Church, but also in sister churches.

No one knows how numerous they are. They are not an organized movement, like the evangelicals. They have not established any expressed self-identity. They have no name.

Many of them, like Chalmers, covet "evangelical"—not as a name so much as a description of their ministry. They sense the often unknowing yearnings of the people for the good news. They see their task as proclaiming the good news that they read in the Bible and that they have experienced.

"Evangelical" being unavailable, let us label their position "good news." I do not propose that term as a party banner, but simply as a handle enabling us to talk here, in these pages, about their position on "authority."

The term "good news" is taken from Chalmer's weekly question: "What is the good news in this passage, for this people, in this place, at this time." That question, however it may be worded, and however it may be asked, is the center point in their quest for faithfulness. It expresses their rootage on the one side in the Bible, and on the other, in the concrete situation. They see the Bible speaking to the world. What the Bible says is ultimately good news. There may come with it a word of reprimand or stern warning. Behind any necessary rebuke, however, is good news.

"Good news" has arisen and spread through the churches with the renewed commitment to Biblical preaching produced by increased use of the lectionary. The lectionary forces the preacher to look to the Bible not for support for his or her message, but for the message itself. It puts the preacher under the Bible, instead of leaving the Bible as the preacher's chief tool. How many times has the lectionary preacher thought "I would never have picked this text," only to hear from it a word the preacher himself or herself needs to hear, a word that becomes a message to the people also. "Good news" is the acceptance of the Bible as master of their preaching; only thus can they hope to be faithful to the Gospel.

This "good news" position is *not* "the position of the United Church." Indeed, it has no claim to any special place within that tradition; it is one among many. But it certainly is not off on the fringes. Chalmers and many others are comfortable within the main stream of the United Church and the United Church seems comfortable with them. Some other positions, also comfortably within the United Church and sister traditions, would show obvious contrasts, but some differ only slightly.

Whitefield Finney has built his faith and his ministry on unwavering allegiance to a few basic doctrines. They are not, by any means, all that he believes, but they underlie and support all the rest. One of them, stripped to its essentials, is that the Bible is the inerrant word of God. This doctrine, he believes, gives a firm anchor for his faith. On the basis of this, we can call him an "inerrantist."

Finney likes that label. It binds him to a large group of Christians, lay and ministerial, who also believe the Bible to be inerrant, and who honor the label "inerrantist." It is for them a king pin in their quest for faithfulness. That group coincides, in North America at least, pretty well with the self-conscious movement proclaiming itself to be "evangelical."

While all inerrantists share a general belief about the Bible, when it comes to details there is considerable variation. No brief summary will cover the broad inerrancy position, though it is a great deal easier than describing an overall United church position. Instead, I will describe one rather extreme variety of "inerrancy," a specifically fundamentalist one. That will be what we have seen at Lighthouse; we will call it the "firm anchor" position. This is just as arbitrary a name as "good news," proposed only for this present discussion.

Given these understandings, the two positions contrast on a number of points clustering around the idea of "authority." The following are ones that have come out as we have compared Central United Church with Lighthouse Bible Church or Calvary Baptist Church:

1. "Firm anchor" asserts that *everything* which the Bible says is without error. "Good news" asserts that the Bible is infallible specifically on matters of "faith and life."
2. "Firm anchor" asserts the truth of every statement *individually*. This extends specifically to details. "Good news" asserts the reliability of the Bible's central message *as a whole*.
3. "Firm anchor" assumes that the primary function of the Bible is to *make statements*. "Good news" does not deny that there are significant statements in the Bible, but it sees these as only one part of the message, and not the central part.
4. "Firm anchor" sees revelation as centrally in the *text* of the Scriptures. "Good news" sees revelation centrally in the *acts* of God, and supremely in the Incarnation.
5. "Firm anchor" sees doctrine as read directly out of the Bible, at most

a systematic reordering of the content of revelation. "Good news" sees doctrine not as a restatement of biblical material, but as a response to the Bible, to the revelation it records, and to human experience with that revelation.

6. "Firm anchor," in formal statements, tends to magnify one function of Scripture, the revealing of doctrine and discipline, and to exclude or minimize all others. "Good news" explicitly recognizes that the Bible is multi-functional.

7. "Firm anchor" sees a very large part of the Scriptures as prophetic, specifically as foretelling events of the "end-times." "Good news" sees a very much smaller part of the whole as prophetic, and less of that as dealing with the consummation of all things.

8. "Firm anchor" is commonly thought of as being literalistic. Actually, except for "end-times" prophecy, all varieties of "inerrancy" frequently take a less literal interpretation than does "good news." "Good news" is more likely to pass over a passage as difficult or unclear in meaning than to use freer kinds of interpretation to force a satisfactory meaning anyway.

9. "Firm anchor," in practice, assumes that the meaning of any Scripture passage is evident to any careful reader. "Good news" recognizes that there are many difficult passages, but that the central message is understandable to ordinary people.

10. "Firm anchor" has traditionally been suspicious of academic work on the Bible, and has attempted to isolate itself from academic research. "Good news" is in theory open, but in practice often a bit puzzled as to the relevance of some scholarly results.

11. "Firm anchor" looks in the Bible for an unchangeable message which retains its validity from community to community and time to time. "Good news" sees the message of the Bible as adapting to the needs and anxieties of any people, situation, and time.

12. "Firm anchor" expects acceptance of the Bible will lead to saving faith. "Good news" believes that the Bible should be read from the standpoint of faith, and within the embrace of the people of God led by the Spirit.

13. "Firm anchor" typically rests the authority of the Scriptures solely on the fact of their composition under inspiration. "Good news" sees the power of the Scriptures as derived from inspiration throughout a process which includes their original creation, editing, and canonization.

14. "Firm anchor" sees the authority of any given book associated with

the author of that book and the author's commission from God. "Good news" sees the specific authorship of any book as a minor consideration.

15. "Firm anchor" commonly ascribes the authority of the Scriptures to the now-lost original texts. "Good news" is confident that the texts we have can be, and are being, used by the Spirit to speak in this day, to present Christ, and to set forth all that is necessary of the Biblical message.

16. "Firm anchor," when it seeks to consider a passage in context, tends to look at series of short passages running through the Old and New Testaments (commonly as set forth in "chain reference Bibles"). "Good news" looks at context in terms of the structure of the canon: first within the book and its internal organization, then within related books, then within the Testament, and only finally in the interaction of the two Testaments. These methods reflect two views of the way passages share in the authority of the whole Bible.

17. "Firm anchor" sees the authority of the Bible as ruling over all people. "Good news" sees the Bible as addressed primarily to the faithful and those who would seek faithfulness. To the faithful it speaks with its own special form of authority. To those outside the church it speaks primarily to invite.

Many in the United churches would stand with "good news" on most of these points, but would wish to modify, restate, remain non-committal, or even side with "firm anchor" on one or more of them. Similarly, most evangelicals would agree with "firm anchor" on most of these points, but would want to modify, restate, or be non-committal on one or more of them. However, the list as a whole can be taken as indicating the *general kinds* of difference that you would find between the larger part of the people of the United churches and the great majority of the evangelicals.

However, we must remember that there is an overlap between the United Church and evangelicalism. Those who own both allegiances find themselves somewhere between the two positions, and would side with "firm anchor" on one point and with "good news" on another—and might differ from both on yet another. Many such intermediate positions can also fit comfortably within the United Church, and other United church people should have no trouble accepting them.

Valuable as such a list may be in clarifying the contrasts, there are certain dangers. One of them is that there is a specious appearance of completeness. The points listed are those that have arisen as we have looked at Lighthouse Bible Church, Central United Church, the town of Springfield, and certain very limited themes in their background. A more complete inspection of those two churches, and of others, might very well have called other points to attention.

Certainly there are some important biblical issues I have barely touched on: the relation of the Old Testament to the New, for example.

There is also a certain inevitable one-sidedness in such a comparison. "Firm anchor" is presented largely in terms of what certain inerrantists assert. "Good news" is seldom clearly formulated, and so is presented more in terms of what can be deduced from preaching, conversation, and observation. Indeed, the list has been drawn up largely on the basis of the "firm anchor" position; then a "good news" response has been added.

A list is hardly the best way to present such differences. Each deserves some detailed explanation; a two-sentence comparison may often be too blunt and too absolute. However, if you think back to what we have related about Lighthouse Bible Church and Central United Church you will see that they have all been exemplified and put in context. They are similarly exemplified in a multitude of communities across Canada and the United States.

Some points of difference cannot be so easily summarized, so I have not attempted to list them. But some of these other points have also been brought out in my comparison of the two churches.

Inerrancy, as its name suggests, starts from the Bible text and a conviction about the Bible. That leads to faith. Faith in the Bible undergirds faith in God and Christ.

This straightforward reliance on the Bible is understood by everyone in churches like Lighthouse. It gives them all a firm anchor and a bond of unity.

However, because it grounds everything on the text, inerrancy becomes its own worst enemy. The most telling argument for it is also the most telling against it: The Bible must be inerrant because, if there is any error even in the most minor and inconsequential point, its whole credibility is destroyed and it is left with no authority for the faith that rests on it.

Inerrancy is like a dike around a city in a time of flood. Any minute crack will let water through, the flowing water will erode the crack into an uncontrollable breach, and very quickly the dike will fail massively. A dike with just one such failure is no dike at all. The problem for inerrantists is that the water is rising so fast that they are having a difficult time keeping ahead, sandbagging the dikes. They are running out of thumbs to plug the small leaks until they can be properly patched.

Inerrantists have tried to contain that danger. One way is by elaborate harmonization. This can lead to deadening concern with the letter and neglect of the spirit. Another is by pushing inerrancy onto the original manuscripts. By so doing, they can assure themselves that, if some difficulty in our present text can not be explained away, it is probably a textual matter. The originals would have had it right. That ascribes the authority, ultimately, to what we do not have and have little hope of finding.

"Good news" is, I believe, more robust. It is scarcely damaged by the myriad of small difficulties that challenge inerrancy. It is more a matter of faith and less of reason. It stands beside Paul when he declares "faith should not stand in the wisdom of man, but in the power of God." (1 Corinthians 2:5) It is, in this sense, more biblical. As I read the Bible, this "good news" position seems to me consistent with how the Bible speaks and how the Spirit speaks.

"Good news" starts, I also believe, from the centrality of Christ, not as a doctrine but as a person. It sees salvation, too, not as a doctrine but as a personal relationship with Christ and his body, the church. It sees the Bible primarily as that which presents Christ—invites, introduces, and reveals his nature. It sees the Bible as a book we get into not simply by our own power but by grace and faith, grace involving the Holy Spirit's speaking to us and our faith answering. It sees the Bible as a book always fresh, one for both the ordinary person and the scholar—as one where the ordinary person and the scholar can meet.

Indeed, it is a book that demands that all sorts of people meet around it; it is a book for the whole people of God. Here is the weak point in the "good news" position: we do not have in the United Church, or most sister churches, the will and the mechanism for deep and meaningful Bible study—not by the adult members and certainly not on an "intergenerational" basis. So it is left to the preacher, alone, to look for the good news addressed to the whole church.

Having said that, I look back on my experiences in churches that claim to be inerrantist. They have been various, of course. I have occasionally gone away from church saddened or disappointed. But that has happened in United churches too.

In most services, however, I have felt something genuine, something that resonates with the Gospel. When I listen carefully to the preaching, I find that it is often only language that marks the best of it off from the best in the United Church. For the most part, we preach the same Gospel because we have read it in the same Book, and have been led by the same Spirit.

The Gospel has taken hold of us all, in spite of our efforts to create divisions among ourselves. Specifically, it has taken hold of us in spite of what we assert about the "authority of the Bible." I need nothing more to convince me of the power of that Gospel.

Inerrancy mars people's reading chiefly when they read disputatiously, to prove their position or to combat another. When we read that way, our reading is marred too.

No matter what doctrinal position we take, when we read *listening*, we hear much the same words, and behind them the Word.

Let us listen.

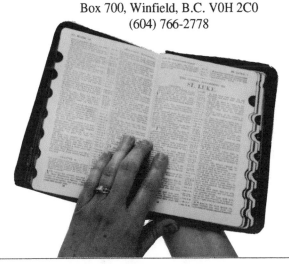

If you enjoyed
Encounters with the Bible
you'll enjoy other
Wood Lake
books

Wood Lake Books is a Canadian Ecumenical
Publisher. Wood Lake specializes in materials for
lay people that cover many subjects such as art,
autobiography, environmental concerns, parenting,
social issues, outreach, human relationships. Wood
Lake publications deal positively and responsibly
with life and faith. To obtain a current catalogue of
Wood Lake's books, which you can then get from
your favorite supplier, please send your name and
address to:

Wood Lake Books
Box 700
Winfield, B.C. V0H 2C0
(604) 766-2778